THIS WAS FORMERLY A PORT CALLED BLAKENEY AND CLEY

Also by

Jonathan Hooton

The Glaven Ports: A Maritime History of Blakeney, Cley and Wiveton in North Norfolk
(Blakeney History Group) 1996

THIS WAS FORMERLY A PORT CALLED BLAKENEY AND CLEY

Important Dates in the Maritime History of the Glaven Ports

Jonathan Hooton

POPPYLAND PUBLISHING

This edition 2021 published by Poppyland Publishing, Lowestoft, NR32 3BB.

www.poppyland.co.uk

ISBN 978 1 909796 81 2

Designed and typeset in 10.5 on 13.5 pt Gilgamesh Pro.

Printed by Ashford Colour Press.

Picture credits (where two images appear on the same page the reference number is shown in brackets):

Acheson, G 65, 78.
Author's collection 2, 8, 13, 17, 22, 34, 35, 37, 39 (8), 42, 49, 51, 60, 67, 68, 69, 70, 75, 82 (40).
Bailey, J 4, 15, 46, 56 (both).
Bensley, M cover, 23 (11), 26, 72, 73, 74 (both).
Blakeney Area History Society (BAHS) 23, 54, 71.
Cooke, D 6.
Creative Commons, 45 (17).
Kadwell, P 32.
Leeds Museums and Galleries/Bridgeman Images 59.
Martin (Creative Commons) 77 (37).
Microsoft Corporation 23 (4), 71.
Norfolk Historic Environment Service 49.
OpenStreetMap contributors (CC BY-SA 2.0) vi.
P. Catling collection 10, 20 (9), 30 (15), 39 (16), 64, 77, 76, 77 (36), 81, 82 (41), 83 (both), 84 (both), 85 (both), 86 (both).
Poppyland collection vi.
Royal Museums Greenwich (Creative Commons) 45 (18).
Sayers, G 25.
unknown 2.
VollwertBIT, I (Creative Commons) 20 (8).
Wolf, J (Creative Commons) 30 (14).

Contents

Map of Evidence Boxes

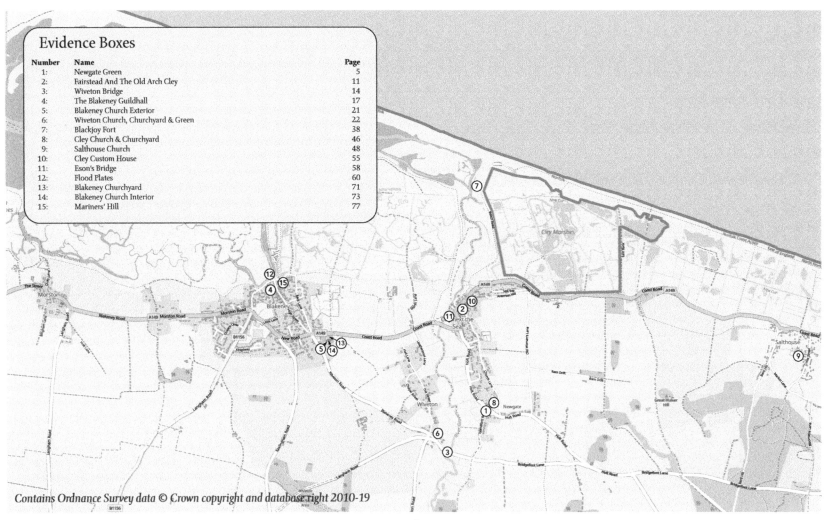

Evidence Boxes

Contains Ordnance Survey data © Crown copyright and database right 2010-19

Preface

WHEN I first visited Blakeney and Cley I was naturally captivated by the settlements, but along with their charm and beauty, I was also puzzled how places, with such small and narrow channels, had ever been thriving ports in the Middle Ages. When, as part of my Geography degree at Cambridge, an opportunity came to research a topic for my dissertation, I chose the decline of the ports of the Glaven Valley. After some fieldwork in the area, and a trawl through some of the more obvious sources, I soon found enough information to complete my dissertation, but was left with much more than the 8,000 words required and many unanswered questions. This led to further research and discussions with others interested in the topic, in particular, two local historians, Magnus (Peter) Catling of Cley and Kenneth Allen of Blakeney, who were most knowledgeable and helpful. The result of that research was a book, *The Glaven Ports*, published in 1996 with the help of the Blakeney Area Historical Society.

Since the publication of that book, I have become increasingly aware of the need to make this information more widely available and this book is the culmination of that effort. While covering essential information found in *The Glaven Ports*, I have included supplementary facts, many of which have come to light in the intervening twenty years. It provides an outline of the maritime history of the area structured around key dates in the development and subsequent demise of the ports. In addition, the "Evidence Boxes", found throughout its pages, guide the reader to some of the surviving relics that can still be seen today.

I hope the result is a comprehensive guide to the maritime past of the Glaven and provides answers to some of the questions, I longed to know, when I first became interested in the area.

Jonathan Hooton, 2021.

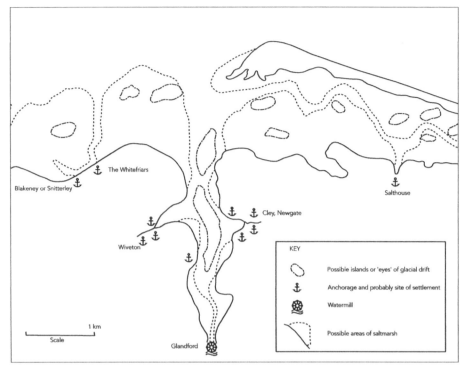

Map 1: Conjectural map of the Glaven Valley AD 1200.

Plate 1: Flooded Estuary—Cley looking south 1 February 1953.

Plate 2: A view across the Glaven from the coast road after the 1953 surge showing what the medieval valley would have looked like at high tide.

1: The Physical Background

IF you look at the east coast of the British Isles, with the exception of Norfolk, it has a largely north-south trend, broken here and there by major estuaries like the Humber and the Thames and a series of minor outlets. The tidal pattern and the direction of the dominant north easterly wave (the one with the longest fetch) create the longshore drift that slowly moves the beach material in a southerly direction.

The Norfolk coast however, is a major exception jutting out in a west-east trend. It has probably formed along the route of a major river channel that ran in this direction before the Ice Age, whose presence was discovered in a series of boreholes drilled along this coast. It is thought that this river's route was probably caused by a west-east fault formed in the underlying basement rocks. Whatever the origins of this river bed, before the Ice Age, it was fed by tributaries on either side. The Ice Age changed all this. Ice sheets moving down from the north completely removed all trace of the tributaries from the northern side. Where the ice sheet ended (roughly parallel with the present Norfolk coast) it covered up any southerly tributaries under a large terminal moraine of material bulldozed by the ice sheet and left after melting. This moraine is the Cromer-Holt ridge, forming the cliffs that run from Happisburgh to Weybourne. However, the former northery flowing tributary rivers remained and now have been re-occupied by rivers like the Glaven, Stiffkey and Burn.

During the Roman occupation when sea levels were higher than at present, they formed wide shallow estuaries that would flood at high tide, giving a safe anchorage inland. The river Glaven was one of these valleys. The Glaven is not a long river and flows for just 17 kilometres from its sources in the Bodham and Baconsthorpe area. It flows in a south-westerly direction towards the headwaters of the Bure before taking a dramatic turn northwards at Hunworth, possibly because a former course was blocked by outwash deposits from a past glaciation. It then makes its way to the North Sea through a valley that begins to widen into a narrow flood plain north of Glandford. It is this floodplain that created the estuary which would have been regularly flooded at high tide. This would have produced ideal sheltered areas for boats around the inlets to the north of Wiveton church and the area south of Cley church, now known as Newgate Green (see plate 3). The Glaven valley once more took on this appearance on the night of 31 January 1953 when it was inundated by the flood water of the storm surge. This water was then trapped behind the flood banks and, as the morning of the 1 February began to dawn, this estuary was once again flooded as far inland as Glandford (see plates 1 and 2).

Plate 3: View of Newgate Green looking north east towards the church; possibly the original site of the port.

EVIDENCE BOX 1: NEWGATE GREEN

ALTHOUGH there is little hard evidence, common sense dictates that the original site for the port of Cley was the triangular green in front of the church known as Newgate Green. It would have been a sheltered inlet off the wide medieval estuary, ideal for beaching fishing boats. Other evidence for this being the original site of the port is the siting of the church nearby, now a kilometre away from the centre of the village, and the fact that house foundations were discovered during road widening in the area, indicating that it was at one time more populous. As late as the 18th century the pub here, now called the *Three Swallows*, had a nautical flavour, being called the *Anchor*. Its changed name had nothing to do with ornithology, but came about after Catherine Swallow became its owner in 1723. Newgate Green was also not the original name of this former inlet, it being named after Christopher Newgate, a wealthy 16th century merchant who lived in what is now called Newgate farm further up the Holt Road. It used to be known as Cley Suggate (or Southgate), to distinguish it from Cley Northgate (the area between the Old Hall and the George and Dragon) and Cley Fleagate (or Fleetgate), the area in between, which lay beside the channel or fleet.

The view across the Glaven valley from Newgate Green would have been very different for most of the past. It would have been a broad estuary with the valley floor flooded at high tide as far inland as Glandford. Since the spit would not have grown across the mouth of the estuary until the late medieval period, the inland sites provided more shelter and were probably the first anchorages.

At high tides the present valley floor would have disappeared under the water and William Cooke, a previous owner of Glandford mill (the head of navigation since at least Domesday) remembered that before the building of the Enclosure bank in 1824 the depth of water at Glandford mill during ordinary spring tides was from four to five feet and the highest he could remember gave a depth of nine feet. Since the fall of water was only six feet, he went on to say 'the current or tidal water has been known to pass through the water-wheel into, or to form a level with, the mill dam'.

This can be more easily visualised in the aerial photograph taken a day after the Storm Surge of 1953 (see plates 1 & 2) when the tidal surge water of the night before became trapped behind the Enclosure bank where the modern coast road is. This briefly returned the Glaven to its medieval appearance although it must be remembered that the photograph was taken looking towards the south.

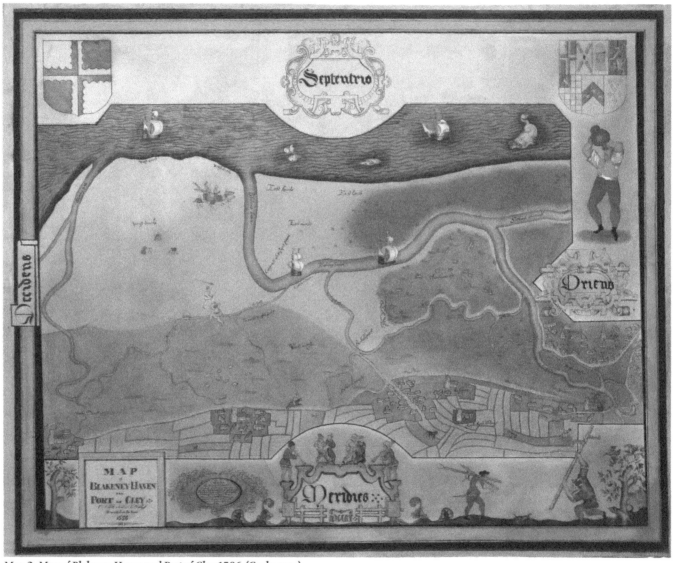

Map 2: Map of Blakeney Haven and Port of Cley 1586 (Cooke copy).

2: The Earliest Map

THE earliest map of the ports is dated 1586 and sheds much light on the way the port developed and is worth considering in detail. The original does not exist, or has been lost. However, there were two copies made of it in 1846 known as the Cooke copy and the Long Copy and although not identical, they are remarkably similar, suggesting that they closely resemble the original. It seems that the map was drawn to help settle a dispute as to whether the Manor of Wighton or the Manor of Cley had the right of wreck on Stiffkey sands. The evidence for this is firstly the date of the map, which is the same year that the commission about the right of wreck first sat. Secondly, that the area in question was sand 'between a place called Stifkey Goate on the west and blakney haven on the east', and the map is bounded on the west by "Stewkey goate" (a goate was a narrow channel of water from the same origin as gate or opening) and to the east, by a channel called "Blakeney Haven" on the map. This would also explain why a map of the ports would have Cley and Wiveton placed on the periphery, rather than occupying a more prominent position in the centre where the sands in question are located. The third piece of evidence is a reference in the Order Book of the Duchy of Lancaster regarding a date for a hearing which mentions that 'the platte (i.e. map or plan) of the sandes or lands in variance already made' should be available. For further information, the reader is referred to *The Glaven Historian* 1 (1998) and my article, '1586 Map of Blakeney Haven and Port of Cley: Part 1' and *The Glaven Historian* 2 (1999) the article, '1586 Map of Blakeney Haven and Port of Cley: Part 2' by John Wright. There is also an online article about the map under publications/online publications at www.bahs.uk (Blakeney Area Historical Society website).

The map is unsigned but there seems little doubt that it was the work of John Darby. Illustrations, almost identical to some on the Blakeney map appear surrounding maps of Aldeburgh (1594) and a Smallburgh Estate map (1582) both of which were signed by John Darby. The evidence for Darby being the cartographer is fully discussed by Raymond Frostick in 'A 16th Century East Anglian Surveyor, and Peter Breugel' in the *Journal of the International Map Collectors' Society* no. 101 Summer (2005).

The version of the map, illustrated in this book as map 2, is the copy made in 1846 and owned by the Cooke family. Another clue that this is the "platte", drawn to accompany the dispute, is that on the sands in question there is a pictorial representation of a wreck being dismantled for profitable salvage (on the area called the west meales to the left of the channel called Blakeney Haven). The legal conflict may also be represented by the illustration of the two characters fighting, found across the stream marked 'the fresh' near the centre of the map.

What does the map tell us about the state of the coast? The most obvious difference from the present day is the length of the spit. Blakeney Point is only shown as reaching as far west as the village of Morston, whereas today Blakeney Channel issues out to sea more to the north of Stiffkey. Other striking differences are to be seen on the channel leading to Cley. There is a broad channel joining the Glaven from the east marked as 'Salthouse Channell' which no longer exists. It flowed from Salthouse north of Cley Eye and was choked out of existence around 1850 as the spit was gradually pushed inland by a series of tidal surges. A process that continues to this day. When the channel did reach Cley, we see that it split into two channels, visible at low tide, called 'Holfleet' and 'Milstead', which briefly joined together to the west of Newgate Green. They then divided, before being crossed by the stone bridge on the Wiveton side and a wooden bridge on the Cley side, joined by a causeway and probably only passable at low tide. The processes working on the coast were the same as today, but the longshore drift had not had enough time to build Blakeney Point as far to the west as at present, and the shingle ridge was further out to sea, allowing a broad channel to Salthouse to exist. Also missing were large areas of reclaimed marsh, although all this was about to change in the 50 years following the drawing of the map.

Plate 4: Figures breaking up a ship from the 1586 map.

What were the differences on land? Cley is shown as the bigger settlement, with a much greater density of housing near the church than at present. It has expanded further north along the channel all the way to where the present windmill is situated. This shift in the economic centre of the village would have been precipitated by a fire that took place 26 years after the map was drawn. Cley church is similar to the present building except for a spire. There is no surviving evidence of the collapse, or dismantling of, a spire, even though it is shown on both of the Victorian copies. It is also strange that, in Blakeney, the second tower is missing. It is marked on one of the map copies, but looks as though it was added later. Blakeney church is drawn in the manner of a standard cartographical symbol and does not show its southern aisle, but does add a nonexistent southern porch. Cley, however, shows the aisles, porches and transepts accurately and even correctly offsets the tower to the north. It includes the clerestory windows and the crosses on the nave and chancel roofs. The Friary church in Blakeney is also shown, which must have still been standing, even though it had not been used since the Reformation fifty years earlier. In drawing any conclusions, we must remember that the purpose of the map was to illustrate the area of the sands that was in dispute and not the settlements.

The channel leading to Blakeney is called 'Benhaugh Streame'. In a statute of 1357, concerning the regulation of the sale of fish at the Blakeney fair, it stated that fish could only be landed here for sale—'betwixt Benorde and Hogfleet'—which probably refers to the channels called Benhaugh and Holfleete on this map and therefore limiting the sale of fish to just the ports of Blakeney and Cley. There is also a solitary building marked on the marshes, in an area known as Thornham' Eye (or island). This indicates the building referred to as 'Blakeney Chapel' whose foundations were excavated recently. The area is shown being grazed by rabbits and a shepherd/warrener, with maybe a ferret on a lead, is keeping a watchful eye on them. Certainly coney skins have been recorded in the port books as an export.

Which side won the dispute is not recorded and the map stayed in the area probably as a status symbol for Sir Christopher Heydon, whose coat of arms is prominently displayed in the top left hand corner. By 1846, when the surviving copies were made, it was recorded that 'this map is in the Possession of the Thomlinson family, to whom the Cley Manor has long belonged'. JW Thomlinson died in 1835 and the house was sold in 1839 when the original map disappeared.

3: Medieval Growth and Prosperity
Fish, Piracy & War

IT was during the medieval period that the importance of the ports became established. The majority of the documentary evidence that has survived for this period comes from the Court Rolls of the Royal Household and is dominated by three themes; fish, piracy and war. Fish, to be more precise, salted fish, was an important part of the medieval diet and played a major part in the purchases of the Royal Household. The North Sea was an important source of fish and most of the ports were engaged in fishing and curing fish and the Glaven estuary was not an exception. Therefore there are several documents referring to the regulation of the fish trade. The North Sea was also a fairly lawless stretch of water and the economic rivalry between the countries bordering it led to many acts of piracy and the court records are full of attempts to settle the disputes and in trying to bring the culprits to justice. There was no Royal Navy during this period. Should the King wish to wage war against a foreign country then he had to rely on the mercantile fleet to provide his warships, troop carriers and to supply the logistics for transporting the armaments and provisions that a successful army fighting abroad would need. Therefore there were endless requests and demands to commandeer vessels to act in the King's service. It is documents such as these that indirectly supply what we know about the ports and their trade and this inevitably gives a biased viewpoint. It is not until the Tudor period that economic documents are more likely to survive and provide more detail about the character of the trade, the ships and people involved with it.

1086 Several authors, including HC Darby[1], note that there appears to be mention of a "port" in the entry for Claia, an outlying estate of the manor of Holt in Domesday Book. This could be the first reference to merchant shipping in the Glaven. However, it is now generally regarded that the word in question is "porc" and not "port" being an abbreviation for pig. Blakeney is not mentioned in Domesday, or, at least, not under its present name. The other outlying estate is termed "Esnuterle" or "Snuterllea", the settlement more commonly known as Snitterley, which gradually became Blakeney, although Domesday gives no indication of any mercantile activity connected with the settlement. The *English Dictionary of Place Names* gives the derivation of Snitterley as coming from a personal name, 'Snytra' the 'leah', or, clearing belonging to 'Snytra' (the wise one), whereas the meaning of Blakeney comes from Black Island, and, therefore, was probably the name for the Point. In historical documents, the term Blakeney is more commonly used in connection with maritime matters and the haven, whereas Snitterley is reserved for issues more usually connected with the settlement on land. It is quite likely that, as the port functions grew in importance, the name of Blakeney (originally reserved for the port) gradually transferred itself to the whole settlement and Snitterley became obsolete.

1223 Over one hundred years later, and still no mention of a port, but in this year Henry III granted Peter de Melton, the privilege of holding a weekly market at Snitterley and an annual fair on St. Nicholas's day—the saint to whom Blakeney church was dedicated and the patron saint of fishermen.[2] This, at least, indicates a healthy level of trade.

Plate 5: The Old Arch and the Queen Victoria (known as the Hole in the Wall) late 19th century.

EVIDENCE BOX 2: FAIRSTEAD AND THE OLD ARCH CLEY

ACCORDING to village tradition, the arch, which appears to be early 14th century, came from the chapel on Blakeney Eye and is shown in this 19th century photograph (plate 5) of Queen Victoria public house employees. The public house was known locally as the 'Hole in the Wall', presumably because of its location next to the arch. (The Holt Licence Registers show the public house closed around 1902/03.) Blakeney Eye, also known in the past as Thornham's Eye, is an island of higher glacial material immediately to the west of the river Glaven as it swings westwards behind the shingle spit. It used to be accessible from the footpath that ran around the marshes from Cley to Blakeney. It has now been cut off by the new channel for the river Glaven, cut by the Environment Agency in 2005/6, to divert the Glaven westerly a further 200 metres inland as the old course was being choked with shingle. Every time there was a tidal surge that overtopped the shingle bank, it would push the bank further inland and was starting to block the old channel, ironically called the 'new cut', as it too had been artificially created in 1924 to prevent the channel being blocked with shingle. It was this gradual move of the shingle spit inland that had previously obliterated the channel that once led to Salthouse, finally closed about 1849.

A secondary benefit of the drainage improvement works carried out by the Environment Agency was that money became available for a full scale archaeological dig on the chapel site, as it was predicted that this would disappear under shingle sometime later this century. The results revealed a late 14th–early 15th century building that had had substantial time and money spent on it, but there was no firm evidence that it was an ecclesiastical building, despite it being described, in 1596, as an 'old house called the Chapel'. Neither was there evidence to refute that claim; and more to the point, measurements taken show that the old arch in Cley would fit exactly into the width of the west entrance of the building. It is also interesting to note that there is a western extension to the current parish boundary, which includes all of Blakeney Eye into the parish of Cley. The remains of this building were re-buried after the dig, but the uneven ground on the 'Eye' gives away its position to the discerning eye.

The footpath through this arch was moved in the 1970s and you now walk through a modern arch a little to the east. If this route is taken, it will lead up to the broader road known as the Fairstead. This road has all the hallmarks of a much wider space, possibly a market area that has been encroached on over the years. The name would indicate that it once was the fair site. The Charter Rolls for 1253 show that Cley was granted a weekly market on a Friday and a yearly fair on the vigil, feast and morrow of St Margaret, to whom the church is dedicated. This fair continues to the present. The *Norwich Mercury* for 6–16 June 1753 confirms this stating that it will still be held on the Saint's day, 19 July 'new stile' ie. as a result of the loss of 11 days caused by adopting the new Gregorian calendar the autumn before. To reflect the decline of this area since its medieval heyday, the Enclosure Act of 1823 moved the fairground to Newgate Green in front of the church. However, it is rational to assume that Fairstead was the site of medieval fairs. The narrow lanes that run down the hill towards the present coast road reflect narrow medieval burgess plots and the remains of long, narrow medieval warehouses and, later, maltings are still evident in places. In medieval times, it is quite likely that the frontages of the dwellings and shops faced the Fairstead, with the workshops, warehouses and workers' quarters ,more likely to be at flood risk, stretching downhill towards the quays and landing places. The remains of one or two of these narrow passageways, such as Post Office Loke, has led Professor Hoskins to speculate that this pattern may be a miniature version of the 'Rows' in Great Yarmouth. There may well be some truth in this.

Further reading:

http://www.norfolkpubs.co.uk/norfolkc/cley/cleyqv.htm accessed 21/02/2020

Lee, R (2006) A Report on the Archaeological Excavation of 'Blakeney Chapel' in *The Glaven Historian* vol. 9.

Hoskins, WG (1967) *Fieldwork in Local History* Faber & Faber London p. 154.

1230   This year produces the first documentary proof of a port. Letters were sent to "Ricardus Alani de Blakeney" and "Radulfus de Cleye", amongst others, informing them of the release of a ship no longer needed for the King's service.[3] They were the bailiffs (port officials) and it is interesting to note that the placename Blakeney and not Snitterley was used and that both, Blakeney and Cley, were treated as separate and equally important ports.

1242   Twelve years later, a request was sent to the Viscount of Norfolk regarding the arrest of ships belonging to Snitterley and Morston to allow those that were unable to carry sixteen horses to go free, being too small for use by the King. This was one of the rare times that the place name Snitterley is mentioned in connection with maritime matters.[4] Usually the State Papers use the term Blakeney when referring to the port. Two other such references from the same year refer to Blakeney.[5] One of these is a request to four East Anglian ports to send ships to Dover. Here Blakeney is considered equal in status to Ipswich and Orford having to provide four ships. Only Dunwich (with five) is asked to provide more.

1253   Trade was obviously increasing for in 1253, only 30 years after Blakeney, Cley was granted a weekly market on Fridays and a three day fair on 'the vigil, feast and morrow of St. Margaret', (17 July, still marked by the village fete on the nearest weekend). The choice of Friday for the market may well reflect the importance of the sale of fish, fresh for the fast day.[6]

1288   By this date, Cley appears to be the more important of the Glaven's ports, as revealed in a legal document relating to the jurisdiction of the port and ownership of the right of wreck. The port of 'Cley and Blakeney alias Snitterly' belonged to the Lords of Cley who held the right of wreck and regularly held port courts. The ships of Snitterly, but not Cley, had to supply 60 herring a year to the Lord of the Manor. Fishing seemed important, as ships had to pay 4d a year to trade in the port or just to dry or spread their nets.[7]

1292   The main east west route across the estuary was via the ford at Glandford, a two mile detour inland. An indication of the size of the problem at high tide can be seen from map 3, which gives a conjectural view of the size of the estuary at this time.

An inquiry held during the following century indicated that human nature was little different then from now, for rather than take the long but safe route, people would try to cross the estuary nearer the coast 'at their own peril after the ebb of the sea.'[8] It was for this reason that William Storm of Snitterly had both the channels of the estuary bridged at this time, or soon afterwards, 'for the soul of Hugh his father' and paid for with Hugh's money. The stone bridge at Wiveton, over the western channel, still stands.

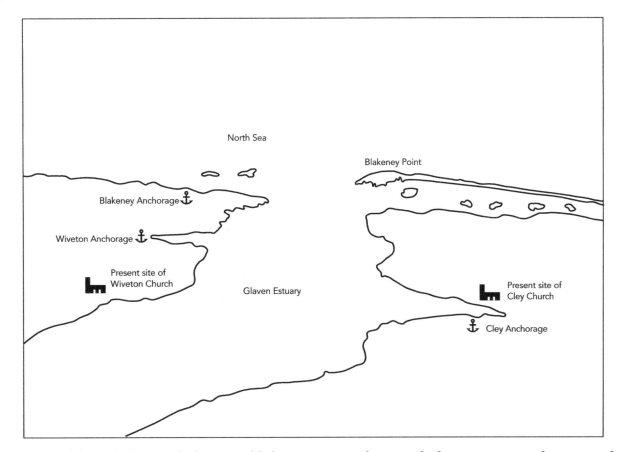

Map 3: A conjectural aerial view of the Glaven estuary during the 13th century.

North Sea

Blakeney Point

Blakeney Anchorage

Wiveton Anchorage

Present site of
Wiveton Church

Glaven Estuary

Present site of
Cley Church

Cley Anchorage

The bailiffs of Blakeney had to supply ships 'suitable for carrying men, horses and other necessaries, and to prepare them with bridges and hurdles, (the addition of raised areas, or castles for the use of fighting men) so as to be with sailors and mariners at Sluys in Flanders on the first Sunday in Lent.'[9]

1298

Three years later, a similar demand requested two ships to join Edward I at Berwick-upon-Tweed to subdue the Scots. Two ships were also required from ports such as London, Bristol and Southampton. Only Lynn (3) and Yarmouth (6) had to provide more.[10]

1301

EVIDENCE BOX 3: WIVETON BRIDGE

AT the time of Domesday, the watermill at Glandford had become the head of navigation and the king's highway crossed the Glaven by a ford, which gave rise to the name and settlement of Glandford. However, in order to avoid the detour via Glandford, people were risking their lives crossing the Glaven estuary here at low tide. It was sometime after 1292 that Thomas Storm, a wealthy Blakeney merchant, built two bridges here 'for the soul of Hugh, his father and with the said Hugh's goods'. Nearly a hundred years after their construction, the bridges were almost impassable, but an inquiry found that, because Thomas had built them 'of devotion and alms', no one was legally responsible for their upkeep. The inquiry also concluded that the stone bridge could be repaired for 20 marks and the wooden bridge for 40 shillings. This provides evidence that the river was braided, and, at low tide, there were at least two large channels which would have been connected by a raised causeway. This is clearly shown on the 1586 map indicating the larger of the two channels was on the Wiveton side of the valley flowing under the stone bridge. It is also interesting to note that the current parish boundary between Wiveton and Cley, which runs down the middle of the Glaven further north, crosses to the eastern side of the valley just north of the bridge, and stays on that side until almost reaching Glandford.

Someone must have thought it worthwhile to repair the bridges since we are left today with a handsome mid-15th century stone structure. The 1586 map (map 2 p. 6) shows it with two arches. Also, at one time, it had a chapel on it. In his will of 1482 Robert Paston of Wiveton leaves 6d for the repair of the chapel of Holy Trinity 'super pontem' ie. on the bridge. Later, in 1508 John Symondes of Cley left 6s 8d to 'The Holy Trinity upon Wyston Brigge'. Could this chapel have been on the buttressed, more substantial, south-western approach, seen on the left hand side of Plate 6?

Standing on top of the bridge the distant western bank helps to visualise how broad the medieval estuary was, although all evidence of the causeway and second wooden bridge have now vanished, nor does any trace of the secondary channel of the river Glaven remain. Looking north along the major channel, it is hard to visualise a bustling medieval port at Wiveton, which, in 1580, owned 13 vessels, 3 of 100 tons and one, the *Marie Grace*, of 120 tons.

Further reading:

TNA: Calendar of Miscellaneous Inquisitions vol. IV no. 124 pp. 76–7.

Hoskins, WG (1967) *Fieldwork in Local History* Faber & Faber London pp. 151–154.

Wright, J (2001) The Bridges of Wiveton in *The Glaven Historian* no. 4 pp. 3–23.

Plate 6: Wiveton Bridge.

1322

Edward II continued where his father left off demanding ships for further campaigns. In 1322, the men of Blakeney had lost their enthusiasm to obey and ignored his demands. The bailiffs were summoned to Lynn and ordered to send a ship to Tynemouth to join a fleet to subdue the Scots. They were still reluctant and in May of that year the bailiffs were ordered, 'to compel all of those towns pertaining to that port' to send a ship provided with armed men. It appears that this time they complied with the order, but, as they probably feared, this was not sufficient and, in June, a further twenty ships were demanded, the Glaven's share being 'two ships in addition to the ship previously granted.'[11]

1326

In 1326 Edward II was preparing to fight the French and Blakeney was included in a list of ports that had to send all ships of over 30 tons with provisions 'for a month at least' to assemble at the Orwell estuary. Later that year another twelve ships were demanded, Blakeney's share being four, to provide a defensive squadron to remain off the coast 'for the repulse of the King's enemies'. They were to be chosen from the better ships of their towns and, in addition to their mariners, had to carry forty armed men.[12]

1335

The continual demands for ships, men and victuals, at times, pushed the goodwill of the merchants and mariners of Blakeney to the limit and they over-reacted in 1335. A ship had been arrested and converted for use in the King's service, but this proved to be too much to bear. A group of men, including several prominent citizens and officials, 'forcibly entered the ship in the said port, sawed through and broke it up, and assaulted the King's men and servants appointed to the custody and governance thereof'. The 'breaking up' would have been restricted to the fore and aft castles and any other adaptations for military service. The main body of the ship would have been left intact as their action was to demonstrate annoyance at the continual loss of their ships for trade. It is not recorded what action was taken by the commission that was set up to enquire into this act of defiance.[13]

1343

A few years later, in 1343, the order was given to arrest Adam Wolstan, and his ship *La Nicolas of Blakeneye*, amongst others. They had all gone to Brest transporting the King's army to France and had been ordered to wait there for further orders. The masters of the ships obviously resented this enforced idleness and a group of them, including Adam Wolstan, decided to depart without permission. Again, the outcome is not recorded and it is not known whether Adam got away with his disobedience.[14]

1347

Only four years later, Blakeney contributed two ships and 38 mariners to the 'huge fleete of Edward the third' that went to lay siege to Calais, apparently without any argument.[15]

1350

It is difficult to assess the relative importance of Blakeney at this time compared with Lynn and Yarmouth. It was not a Head port like the other two, but it was obviously an important enough harbour to be the centre of squabbles over whether it should be included within the influence of the Custom Houses at Yarmouth or Lynn, lying as it does, almost equidistant between the two. In 1350 Thomas de Drayton and Simon Horn of Yarmouth were ordered, 'not to meddle in the collection of customs and subsidies at the Port of Blakeneye by pretext of the commission lately granted them, as the King wills that the collectors of customs and subsidies in the port of Lenne shall collect at the port of Blakeneye.'[16]

It was around this time that the 'guildhall' was built, the oldest secular building in Blakeney. What remains of this two storey building is a fine brick vaulted undercroft (plate 7). It is likely to have been a merchant's house and is indicative of the wealth of Blakeney during the 14th century. The owner was likely to have earned his fortune trading in fish.

c.1350

Blakeney was the major centre on the north Norfolk coast for the sale of salt fish and buyers from the Royal Household regularly visited the port throughout this century to make large purchases. For example, six years previously (1351) the Black Prince stated that he 'needs a great amount of salt fish to victual his household for his next expedition beyond the sea to war' and he contacted Thomas Storm of Blakeney who was ordered to, 'purvey and purchase in the towns of Blakeneye, Snyterleye, Wyveton, Clay, Salthouse, Shiryngham, Wellles and elsewhere in the neighborhood…up to 1200 lobbe, lieng, talcod and other kinds of saltfish and keep them safely until the arrival of the Prince's said serjeant'. In 1357 an Act of Parliament was passed to regulate the trade and try to prevent the many abuses that had developed. Transactions at the Blakeney fish fair were ordered to take place in the open, in broad daylight and in a prescribed area, 'betwixt Benorde and Hogfleet and in none other place'. These

1357

EVIDENCE BOX 4: THE BLAKENEY GUILDHALL

This Grade II* listed building can be found to the left of the High Street just in front of Mariner's Hill. A single room remains, which is believed to be the undercroft of a medieval merchant's house. It is presumed, at one time, to have had another two storeys above the present structure. The brick vaulted ceiling, supported on three octagonal stone piers, is thought to be mid-14th century, although Historic England now believe it might be 15th century, with the listed building register describing the walls as having, 'been dated to the 15th century'. In the south eastern corner is a projecting rectangular structure which contains the remains of a garderobe shute from the upper level. It has always been known as the Guildhall, although there is, as yet, no evidence that it was anything more than a merchant's basement or warehouse for the storage of goods. In the subsequent centuries it has been used for many things. Documents show that it was in the hands of trustees who rented it out as a charity for the benefit of parish. There are indications that it may have been a tavern at one time and workshops at another. A report by the Charity Commissioners in 1834 found it was being used as a coal store for Messrs. Brereton, local corn and coal merchants and ship owners, the rent being 63 bushels of coals, to be delivered each winter to the doors of 63 poor families. The Breretons had been doing this since 1818. However, as the lease could not be found, the Commissioners felt that 63 bushels of coal was

Plate 7: Interior of the 'Guildhall'—a medieval undercroft.

not the true economic value of the store and that it should be let for its full monetary value, to which the Breretons readily agreed.

In more recent times it has been used as a packing store for worm bait, a mortuary for bodies recovered at sea, a mushroom forcing house and a boathouse. It was scheduled as an Ancient Monument in 1924 and, when earth was removed from the east side walls during restoration in 1959, four mullioned windows were discovered. This disproved a theory that the building had been deliberately built into the hill. This also indicated that Mariner's Hill, referred to as 'a mountain called Wellburgh' in a deed of 1677, was at least partly artificial and had been built up since the 14th century. The building's 1924 listing gives one reason for its classification as: 'It is a good example of a high status, urban medieval domestic building in flint and stone, with well-preserved interior brick and stonework and demonstrates the wealth and importance of Blakeney as a port during the medieval period.'

Further reading:

Wright, J (2002) The old 'Guildhall' at Blakeney in *The Glaven Historian* no. 5 p. 66.

https://historicengland.org.uk/listing/the-list/list-entry/1014237.

Pevsner, N &. Wilson, W (1997) *The Buildings of England Norfolk 1: Norwich and the North-East* Yale University Press p. 398.

were the names of the Blakeney and Cley channels, referred to on the 1586 map, and therefore, this clause restricted the trade to the quays of Blakeney, Cley and Wiveton, where it could be regulated. Other details of the Act, and a similar Act relating to Great Yarmouth, indicated a division of trade. Whereas Great Yarmouth specialised in herring, Blakeney was the centre for cod, lob and ling.[17]

1360   There is an intriguing reference in 1360 suggesting that, by this date, the Blakeney fishermen were already travelling to Iceland to catch their cod and ling. In that year a Franciscan friar, Nicholas de Lynna, was said to have made a voyage to 'all the Regions situate under the North pole'. Writing about that voyage, the mathematician, John Dee, noted that it took no more than a fortnight to sail from Lynn to Iceland and that it, 'hath bene of many yeeres a very common and usuall trade: which further appeareth by the privileges granted to the Fishermen of the towne of Blacknie in the said Countie of Norfolke, by king Edward the third, for their exemption and freedome from his ordinary service, in respect of their trade to Island'.[18] However, there is no mention of the English visiting Iceland in the detailed Icelandic annals until 1412, and the Icelandic authority, Bjorn Thorsteinsson, has rejected all evidence for English ventures travelling to Iceland in the 14th century as unreliable.[19]

1376   A dispute over who was responsible for the wreck of the *George* in Blakeney harbour is of interest because of the cargo. It was salt from France. Salt was needed in large quantities to preserve the fish and the best salt came from abroad. One of the people involved in this dispute was Robert Rust, described as a merchant of Blakeney. He appears three years later (1379) as the master of a ship hired to transport a complement of soldiers under the command of Sir John Arundel from Portsmouth to Brittany. When they were due to sail, Robert did not like the look of the weather and advised Sir John to wait until the storm was over. But he was overruled by Sir John who insisted they sailed at once. This proved to be a mistake. After several days, being driven by the weather, they ended up off the coast of Ireland, taking in water. They found a place to attempt a landing but ran aground. Rust and several of the crew managed to leap ashore. However, Sir John landed on quicksand and Rust went to his aid. Whilst he was trying to save Sir John, a large wave washed them both out to sea and they were never seen again.[20]

Although the fish trade dominated the port, during this century other goods are mentioned in the records and smaller quantities of wheat, barley, rye, malt, peas and beans were exported and wine imported.

1394—8

The end of the 14th century was marked by a series of incidents of piracy that was a result of the intense rivalry between the English merchants and the Hanseatic League. An agreement between Henry IV and the Hanseatic merchants to ensure peaceable trade listed twenty-seven instances of robbery and violence, between 1393 and 1405, directed at vessels from the east coast ports for which compensation was claimed. Of these, twelve, or nearly half, involved ships belonging to Cley and Wiveton, or trading for merchants based there. All the ships belonging to the Glaven were fishing vessels, one of which was 'wickedly spoiled' whilst 'lying at anker, while the companie were occupied about fishing'. In addition to stealing the catch, or taking the vessel, the crew were frequently beaten, or, in one case, 'the master and 25 mariners in the same ship they maliciously slew'. The robbery and lawlessness was not a one sided affair and the representatives of the Hanseatic League also claimed for 'sundry other damages, grievances, and robberies' including accusing the 'inhabitants of Scardeburgh, Blakeney, and Crowmer (who had one John Jolly of Blakeney for their captaine)'.[21]

1406

Another example of piracy early in the 15th century was when the *Maryenknight*, travelling from Scotland to France, was attacked by Hugh atte Fen of Yarmouth and Nicholas Steyard of Cley. As well as Scottish wool and hides, they captured the Earl of Orkney and young Prince James, (later to be James I of Scotland) escaping to France. He was taken to London where Henry IV had him imprisoned in the Tower for eighteen years. Both Hugh, a prominent Yarmouth merchant, and Nicholas had suffered at the hands of the Hanse, but this time they were rewarded with the cargo by a grateful Henry IV.[22]

1407—8

Despite royal agreements, relations between the English and the Hanse did not readily improve. In 1412 the Lynn merchants were petitioning the Crown to have members of the Hanseatic League living in Boston bound over for a reasonable sum to ensure that their compatriots kept the peace when trading in England or Norway. Among their complaints was that some four or five years earlier '100 fishermen of Crowmere and Blakeneye and other towns of the coast of Norfolk' fled to the port of Wynforde in Norway where, far from receiving protection, they were set upon by 500 men of the Hanse from Bergen and drowned.[23]

Plate 8: A reconstruction of a Hanseatic cog discovered in the Weser near Bremen thought to date from 1380. This was typical of the vessels trading from Blakeney at this time.

Plate 9: The billyboy 'Angerona' at Cley Mill. This was supposedly the last ship to unload directly at Cley quay and not by lighter. She was a flat bottomed single masted clinker built billyboy showing many similarities to the medieval cog.

With atrocities such as these an ever present threat for the North Sea fishermen, it is not surprising that attempts were made at protection. In 1415, John Broun and Thomas Lytherpole of Wiveton, Philip Lent and Robert de Paston from Salthouse and Robert Herryson of Cley were appointed 'to keep the sea for the protection of fishermen and other lieges of the King … provided they do not take any goods or merchandise of anyone except the King's enemies of France and Scotland'.[24]

1415

The maritime wealth acquired by the inhabitants of the Glaven led to the rebuilding of the churches of the Glaven during this century. A date of 1435, found in the tower at Blakeney, is thought to record the completion of this church. The re-building of Wiveton happened soon after, as did the completion of Cley church, the re-building of which is thought to have been suspended part of the way through the previous century because of the ravages of the Black Death.

1435

EVIDENCE BOX 5: BLAKENEY CHURCH EXTERIOR
(see also Evidence Boxes 13 and 14)

THE chancel is the only surviving part of the original Early English church. The nave and tower were re-built (probably with money from maritime trade) in the new perpendicular style and completed, according to a date in the tower, in 1435. However, the most curious feature, seen from outside, is the unique small second tower besides the chancel. This is also perpendicular in style and probably built at the same time. It seems that the chancel was enlarged when the rebuilding was taking place. Several of the windows were enlarged and filled with 15th century tracery. An upper room was added to the chancel so that its overall size was in proportion to the grand new nave. The second small tower contains a staircase to provide access to this new room.

However, this tower extends well above the chancel roof, which would seem an expensive architectural luxury for a stair turret. This feature has led some to speculate that the tower's extension was designed to serve as a lighthouse for shipping. It has certainly served that purpose and for much of its history a light has been maintained there. The much larger tower would have served this purpose better, unless this was considered an unacceptable fire risk. Its height has certainly been used in daylight hours. During the 19th century a sailor was employed to hoist a flag on the main tower whenever there was sufficient water over the bar to allow ships to enter. It has also been proposed that, when it was built, the entrance to Blakeney harbour was opposite Cley, and that lining up both the towers would guide a ship through the channel between the sand banks. This suggestion must be dismissed because the channels and banks shift so frequently that, had this been the case, when they started building the tower it could well have been obsolete by the time it was finished. Whatever the reason for building the second tower, it is likely that its main use would have been in daylight because it made Blakeney church instantly recognisable, distinguishing it from other church towers visible from the sea.

The dedication of the church is perhaps significant, since St Nicholas was patron saint of fishermen and sailors. Henry III granted Blakeney an annual fair on St Nicholas's day (6 December). This may well have taken place in front of the church, since in an 18th century survey of the parish (by William and Corba Cranefield, dated 1769) the present northern graveyard was called 'Church Green, formerly the market place'.

Further reading:

http://www.heritage.norfolk.gov.uk/record-details?MNF6167-St-Nicholas%27-Church-Blakeney&Index= 2&RecordCount=3&SessionID=12c6c0ef-7727-45f8-94f2-6ddd37a9e878.

EVIDENCE BOX 6: WIVETON CHURCH, CHURCHYARD & GREEN

Plate 10: *Blakeney Church chancel tower*

THE 15th century was prosperous for Norfolk and its ports. Much of this wealth resulted in the rebuilding of their churches. Blakeney had largely been rebuilt by 1435 and the port of Wiveton was not to be outdone by its neighbour. Two years later, John Hakon left 200 marks for building a new church and it seems that this generosity started the rebuilding of Wiveton church in the fashionable perpendicular style, with little of the original church remaining. In the same year as Hakon's will (1437), there is a list in the Patent rolls ordering the release of fishing vessels, which had been detained in readiness for service in the King's navy, allowing them to go to sea (TNA: PRO 15 HENRY VI Feb 28th). Amongst those mentioned are John Hagon (Hakon) from Wevyngton (Wiveton), who possessed one dogger and four lodeships. It shows that the church of Wiveton stands as evidence of the wealth of the port.

The coat of arms of Raulf Greneway (on the wall near the south door) shows an engrailed chevron, between three griffins; on the chevron are two anchors—could this be connected with the port? Ralph Greneway left Wiveton to become a successful Grocer and Alderman in London, but his father was the master of the *Mary of Wiveton*, recorded as taking barley to Newcastle and returning with coal in 1510; his will showed that he came to own six ships and the family's fortunes were, without doubt, founded on shipping.

Further maritime evidence is to be found in the ship graffiti scratched onto the columns. Twelve have been identified, although some are hard to see. The best example is on the pillar on the south east corner of the chancel.

The fine portrait brass of George and Anne Brigg, owner of one of the Wiveton manors, is also connected with the port. Despite George's will expressing the view that Sara, his daughter, should marry her cousin Erasmus Brigg and she was to be disinherited if she chose John Jenkenson of Cley, she married John. Their daughter, Anne, married John Shovell of Cockthorpe and later gave birth to Cloudesley Shovell, who became a famous 17th century admiral. (See evidence boxes 8 and 9.)

Outside the church there are several gravestones with maritime connections (map 4). Perhaps the most interesting are the two Cooper stones opposite the fourth buttress on the southern aisle (which has a scratch dial on it). Both are sailors who, although connected with Blakeney and Cley, were born several centuries after Wiveton ceased to be a port. There was a close connection with the north east ports and several Glaven families moved to Shields to become involved with their ships as trade declined in the 19th century. Dennis Cooper was lost from a North Shields ship, whereas William Cooper was lost from a Cley ship. The *Riga* was a brig owned by William Porritt of Cley. Her size, 177 tons, meant that she never sailed from this port, but obviously had crew from the local area.

Plate 11: *15th century Wiveton. Detail from* The Glaven Ports c1400 *by Mick Bensley. Note Wiveton bridge bottom left leading to a flooded causeway.*

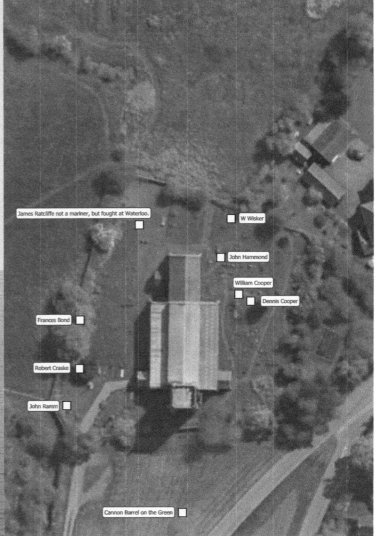

James Ratcliffe not a mariner, but fought at Waterloo.

W Wisker

John Hammond

William Cooper

Dennis Cooper

Frances Bond

Robert Craske

John Ramm

Cannon Barrel on the Green

Map 4: *Plan of Wiveton Church and Churchyard showing maritime connections.*

A look over the eastern churchyard wall shows the valley across to Cley church. In the days when Wiveton was an important port it would have been a broad estuary, flooded at high tides and with two main channels exposed at low tide, which would have hugged the opposite sides of the valley. According to local tradition, there were mooring rings for ships in the churchyard wall until they were removed in the 1970s (See Plate 11). The largest ship belonging to Wiveton mentioned in the records was the *Abraham of Wifton*, burden eight score ton (160 tons) which sailed to and from Hamburg in 1587.

Leaving the churchyard, it is worth inspecting the gun barrel in the middle of the green, which is a reminder that, throughout the Middle Ages and Tudor period, piracy and warfare were never far away. In 1395 the *Peter* of Wiveton, laden with salt fish was captured off the coast of Denmark, the Master and 25 mariners murdered and the ship's boy abducted. This cannon would not have been much use in seeing off enemies as it has a huge hole in the side of the barrel. There is also a cannon ball stuck in the end of it. Perhaps the wrong sized shot was used which got lodged and resulted in the damage. It is probably fanciful, but it would be nice to believe that the gun barrel was left over from the ten pieces of 'cast ordinaunce', recorded in the port books, which arrived from Yarmouth in the *Rose of Claye* in July 1587, the year before the Armada.

Further reading:

Hakluyt, R (1907) *The Principal Voyages, Traffiques and Discoveries of the English Nation* London vol. 1 pp. 139–57.

Ferroussat, M (2000) Wiveton Churchyard: Monumental Inscriptions and Plan of Burials in *The Glaven Historian* no. 3.

Peake, P (2003) A Family of Substance: George Brigg of Wiveton & his relatives in *The Glaven Historian* no. 6.

Peake, P (2012) Ralph Greneway: more than a Myth in *The Glaven Historian* no. 13.

1436   By 1436 there is evidence of a thriving trade with the north European ports and the enmity of forty years before seems largely to have abated. Six foreign merchants were recorded as living in the Glaven valley. They had taken an oath of fealty and the port bailiffs were ordered to allow them 'to inhabit the realm peaceably'. Two were recorded as living in Cley, three in Blakeney and, most curiously, two dwelling in Snitterley. There could not have been two settlements at this date, but it is possible that different areas within the same settlement (possibly those centred on the quay and the Carmelite Friary) were called by different names.[2]

1437   Whatever the level of trade with the Low Countries, it is obvious from the bulk of the documents that fishing was still the major activity. Frequently during this period vessels were prevented from going to sea because they had been 'arrested' (or ordered to wait in readiness) for possible service in the King's navy. In 1437 the authorities relented and allowed a substantial fleet from north Norfolk to 'have free passage to sea' and it goes on to list the vessels, their owners and their places of origin (see table 1).[26]

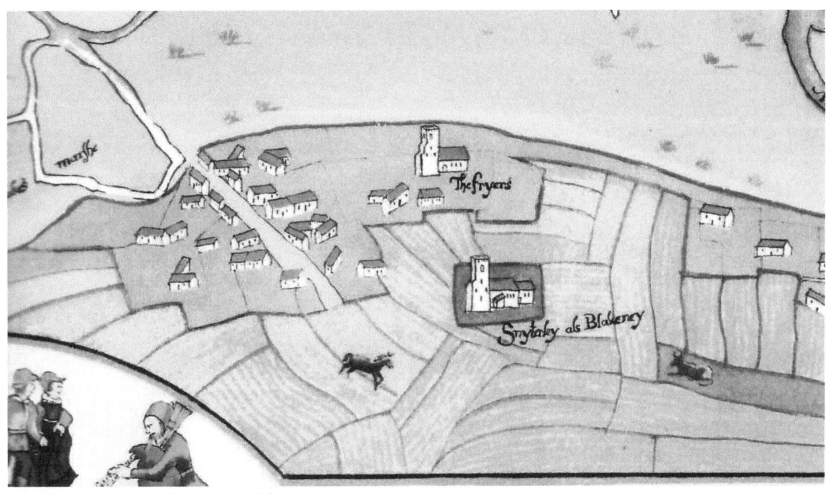

Map 5: a detail from the 1586 map showing the quay and the Friary.

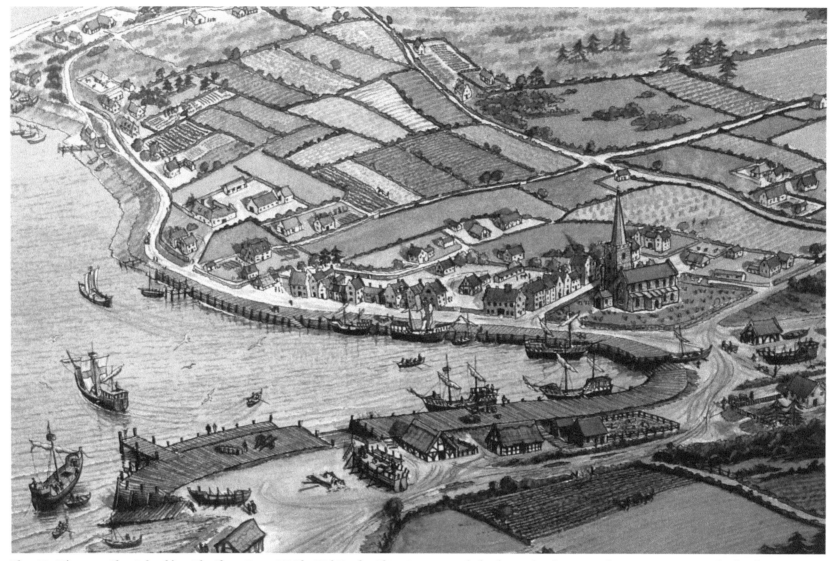

Plate 12: 15th century Cley. A detail from The Glaven Ports c1400 by Mick Bensley. This print imagines the bustling medieval port around Newgate Green next to the church.

Table 1: Norfolk Ships released from Naval service 1437

Port	No. of ships	Port	No. of ships
Cromer	14	Wells	7
Sheringham	3	Holkham	1
Salthouse	1	Burnham	2
Cley	18	Yarmouth	6
Wiveton	6	Lynn	1
Blakeney	7	Dersingham	4

The practice of fishing in convoys is well documented. Only the previous year a licence had been given to the fishermen of the towns of Blakeney and Cromer 'to put to sea with 24 of their vessels appointed for fishing this season, any arrest on such vessels notwithstanding, provided always that their masters keep their vessels continually in company'.[27] It is quite probable that the ships of Cromer, Sheringham and Salthouse, if not others in the list, operated out of the Glaven valley and the first six places mentioned in the first column may have belonged to a fishing convoy.

The first indication of the size of ships using the Glaven comes from records of the fleet assembled at Portsmouth to set sail for Normandy during the 100 Years' War. Blakeney supplied three ships and Cley nine. The tonnages given mainly ranged from 30 to 60 tons, but three ships, the *Margarete* from Blakeney and the *Xpofre* (*Christopher*) and *Jamys* from Cley, were all of 100 tons. Tonnage measurement at this time was not very accurate but there were not many ships larger than this. The biggest were the *Marie* of Boston, 200 tons, and the *Swan* of London, also of 200 tons. That the Glaven Ports could supply three ships of 100 tons is a good indication of a thriving medieval trade and it seems to indicate that Cley was the more important of the Glaven towns.[28]

1442–3

The Blakeney vessels were not confined solely to trading from their own home port but must have been involved in the trade from several of the east coast ports. Evidence of this is found in 1457 when pirates from Calais attacked a Blakeney ship, *Le Julyan*. Its owner, Sir Thomas de Roos, the Lord of the Manor, had been hired by Hanseatic merchants to transport 247 woollen cloths and other goods, valued at £900, from Boston to Norberne in Norway.[29]

1457

The lack of references for the rest of the 15th century does not necessarily reflect a downturn in trade. Most of the evidence for this period comes from the State Papers and refers to acts of piracy, law breaking and war. Any details of trade are quite incidental to the original purpose of the documentation. By 1455, the English had lost every possession in France except Calais and the Wars of the Roses had confined most of the conflict to the mainland. From 1485 onward, Henry VII brought relative peace and prosperity. So the absence of records probably indicates a period of quiet and prosperous trade. Fish was still the major commodity and east coast mariners were sailing further afield to obtain it. It was during this period that the Iceland trade developed.

Notes

1   Darby, HC (1986) In *Domesday England*. Cambridge: Cambridge University Press. p. 350.

2   Blomefield, F (1808) In An essay towards a topological history of the County of Norfolk vol. 9 2nd ed. Cont by Charles Parkin London. p. 362.

3   Great Britain. Public Record Office (19011903) *Patent rolls of the reign of Henry III preserved in the Public Record Office: 1216–[1272]vol. 2* London: Printed for His Majesty's Stationery Office by Mackie and Co. p. 44.

4   Close Rolls of the reign of Henry III. (n.d.) Retrieved 24 November 2020, from https://archive.org/details/closerollsofreig04grea/page/410/mode/2up.

5   Close Rolls of the reign of Henry III. (n.d.) Retrieved 24 November 2020, from https://archive.org/details/closerollsofreig04grea/page/456/mode/2up p. 476.

6   Calendar of the charter rolls: Preserved in the Public Record Office 1226–[1516]: Great Britain. Public Record Office free download, Borrow, and Streaming. (1970, January 01). Retrieved 24 November 2020, from https://archive.org/details/calendarofcharte01grea/page/416/mode/2up.

7   Norfolk Record Society vol. 1 (1931) *Calendar of the Frere mss.* p. 14.

8   Hoskins, WG (1967) In *Fieldwork in Local History*. Faber and Faber Ltd. pp. 151–4.

9   Great Britain (1895) Calendar of the patent rolls preserved in the Public Record Office / prepared under the superintendence of the deputy keeper of the records. 1292–1301 Edward I v.3. Retrieved 24 November, 2020, from https://babel.hathitrust.org/cgi/pt?id=mdp.39015031081154 p. 328.

10   Great Britain (1895) Calendar of the patent rolls preserved in the Public Record Office / prepared under thesuperintendence of the deputy keeper of the records. 1292–1301 Edward I v.3. Retrieved 24 November 2020, from https://babel.hathitrust.org/cgi/pt?id=mdp.39015031081154 p. 635.

11   Stephenson, WH (1895) Calendar of the close rolls preserved in the Public Record Office : Edward II. v.3. Retrieved 24 November 2020, from https://babel.hathitrust.org/cgi/pt?id=umn.31951002067096n pp. 524, 536, 546, 549–50, 670.

12   Stevenson, WH (1898) Calendar of the close rolls preserved in the Public Record Office : Edward II. v.3. Retrieved 24 November 2020, from https://babel.hathitrust.org/cgi/pt?id=umn.31951002067096n p. 613.

13   Great Britain (1895) Calendar of the patent rolls preserved in the Public Record Office / prepared under the superintendence of the deputy keeper of the records. 1334–1338 Edward III v.3. Retrieved 24 November 2020, from https://babel.hathitrust.org/cgi/pt?id=mdp.39015011275826 p. 215.

14   Great Britain (1904) Calendar of the Close Rolls Edward III vol. VII AD 1343–1346 HMSO London. Retrieved 30 November 2020, from https://archive.org/stream/cu31924091767917 p. 132.

15   Hakluyt, R (1907) *Principal navigations voyages traffiques and discoveries of the English nation* (vol. 1,) London: Dent & Sons.p. 98.

16   Great Britain (1921) Calendar of the Fine rolls preserved in the Public Record Office. vol. VI Edward III AD 1347–1356. Retrieved 30 November 2020, from https://babel.hathitrust.org/cgi/pt?id=mdp.39015017688956 p. 243.

17 Great Britain (1933) Register of Edward, the Black Prince, preserved in the Public Record Office / prepared under the superintendence of the Deputy Keeper of the Records. v.4.HMSO London. Retrieved 30 November 2020, from https://babel.hathitrust.org/cgi/pt?id=inu.32000000340044; Statute cap 1 31 Edward III 1357.

18 ibid., 15. p. 100.

19 Thorlaksson, H personal communication.

20 Great Britain (1913) *Calendar of the Close Rolls Edward III vol. XIV /ad 1374–1377*. HMSO London. Retrieved 30 November 2020, from https://archive.org/stream/cu31924091767982 ; Rye, W. A Norfolk Shipmaster 1379–80 Robert Rust of Blakeney *Norfolk Archaeology* vol. 22 (2) pp. 127–32.

21 ibid., 15. pp. 146–57

22 Balfour-Melville, EWM James I, King of Scots London (1936) pp. 30–33; Great Britain. (1907) Calendar of the patent rolls preserved in the Public Record Office / prepared under the superintendence of the deputy keeper of the records. 1405–1408 Henry IV v.3. Retrieved 30 November 2020, from https://babel.hathitrust.org/cgi/pt?id=mdp.39015031079588 p. 168.

23 Great Britain (1909) Calendar of the patent rolls preserved in the Public Record Office / prepared under the superintendence of the deputy keeper of the records. 1408–1413 Henry IV v.4. Retrieved 1 December 2020, from https://babel.hathitrust.org/cgi/pt?id=mdp.39015031079570 p. 384.

24 Great Britain (1910) Calendar of the patent rolls preserved in the Public Record Office / prepared under the superintendence of the deputy keeper of the records. Henry V, 1413–1416. Retrieved 1 December 2020, from https://babel.hathitrust.org/cgi/pt?id=njp.32101076189834 pp. 363–4.

25 Great Britain (1907) Calendar of the patent rolls preserved in the Public Record Office / prepared under the superintendence of the deputy keeper of the records. Henry VI vol. II 1429–1436. Retrieved 1 December 2020 from https://babel.hathitrust.org/cgi/pt?id=mdp.39015031079521&view=2up&seq=576&size=150 pp. 541–88.

26 Great Britain (1907) Calendar of the patent rolls preserved in the Public Record Office / prepared under the superintendence of the deputy keeper of the records. 1436–1441 Henry VI v.3. Retrieved 1 December 2020, from https://babel.hathitrust.org/cgi/pt?id=mdp.39015031079612 p. 42

27 Great Britain (1907) Calendar of the patent rolls preserved in the Public Record Office / prepared under the superintendence of the deputy keeper of the records. 1429–1436 Henry VI v.2. Retrieved 1 December 2020, from https://babel.hathitrust.org/cgi/pt?id=mdp.39015031079521 p. 515.

28 Retrieved 24 January 2020 from http://medievalandtudorships.org/search_ports/?Misc[Home-port]=Cley%20next%20the%20Sea#selected=62,65&range=0,40&selected-categories=Port,Ship,Voyage_origin ; and http://medievalandtudorships.org/search_ports/?Misc[Home-port]=Blakeney#selected=62,65&range=404,444&selected-categories=Port,Ship,Voyage_origin.

29 Great Britain (1910) Calendar of the patent rolls preserved in the Public Record Office / prepared under the superintendence of the deputy keeper of the records. 1452–1461 Henry VI v.6. Retrieved 1 December 2020, from https://babel.hathitrust.org/cgi/pt?id=mdp.39015031079547 p. 348.

Plate 13: Gyrfalcon—although the most common import from Iceland was saltfish, occasionally they brought back the prized Gyrfalcon. In 1598 the 'Susan' of Blakeney returned with 16 hawks 'called Gerfawcons'.

Plate 14: The effect of scour by high tides. Two views of Cley mill. Above: low tide. Below: high spring tide.

4: Tudor Heyday
From Iceland to Crete

THE 16th century was probably the pinnacle of the maritime trade of the Glaven Ports. By the end of this century, they were sending vessels as far as Iceland in the north and to Marseilles and Crete in the south. There was a steady trade to northern Europe and the Baltic states and the Port Books, introduced in 1565, show some years where the overseas trade was greater than the coastal trade. There was a steady number of ships engaged in trade along the coast—exporting grain, malt and other agricultural produce and importing coal, wood and building materials—visiting most of the ports from the north east down to those on the southern coast. The pattern of trade was similar to rival ports. Although in centuries to come there were more vessels using the ports, the number did not increase as much as other ports like Bristol and Liverpool. Unlike these ports, the Glaven was not able to take advantage of the trade across the Atlantic or the southern hemisphere that developed in the following centuries. The Glaven was not deep enough to accommodate the larger deep-sea vessels nor did it have a hinterland accessible from an extensive inland river system. In addition, it was not large enough to supply the capital needed to finance the growing colonial ventures. So the end of the Tudor period marked a relative decline in its maritime importance.

According to legend, a Cromer fisherman, Robert Bacon, discovered Iceland, although it is nonsense to assume that he discovered an unknown isle.[1] For some reason trade with Iceland had ceased during the previous century, which may have been due to a stranglehold placed upon it by Norway. However, by the beginning of the 15th century, possibly due to a relaxation in political control and the migration of fish from the North Sea, the east coast ports once again started to trade with Iceland. It is likely that the Glaven Ports were involved from the start, although the first documentary proof comes from 1438, when Roger Fouler of Cromer freighted a ship for Iceland owned by Adam Horn of Cley.[2] By the beginning of the 16th century it was a major part of the trade.

The importation of coal from the north east was also well established by the start of the 16th century. This was to remain the backbone of the Glaven's trade until its eventual demise, long after fish had ceased to be important. The Newcastle-upon-Tyne Chamberlain's accounts have survived for the period 1508—11 and provide a wealth of detail that illustrates the importance of coal to all the east coast ports.[3] Yarmouth dominated the trade with 305 coal ships leaving Newcastle during this period. The total for all ports in north Norfolk amounted to 264—51 belonging to Blakeney, Cley and Wiveton. Although the majority of these vessels entered Newcastle in ballast, a number arrived with barley and malt, and smaller quantities of wheat, rye and herrings were also exported.[4] Map 6 compares the relative importance of the Glaven Ports with other north Norfolk ports visiting Newcastle in this period.

1508—11

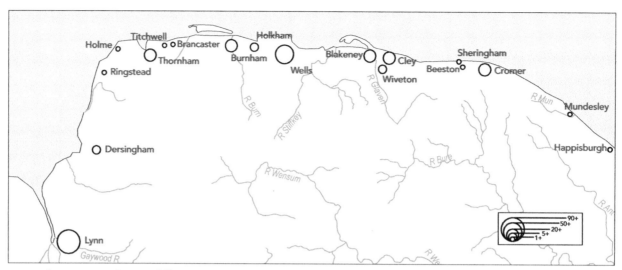

Map 6: Ship movements from Norfolk ports trading with Newcastle 1508–11 (after Fraser).

1522   In 1522, the embanking of the marshes is first mentioned. The marshes, as well as playing an important part in the local economy, were of vital importance to the well-being of the port. At high tides they were flooded with water and, during the ebb, this volume of water draining out to sea flushed any silt out of the channels, keeping them navigable. Any attempt at reclamation would reduce the scouring power of the tide and threaten the viability of the port. One can get an idea of the amount of water involved by comparing the two views of Cley mill in Plate 14.

Sir John Heydon had enclosed some of the marshes in Salthouse and this had obviously had a detrimental effect on land belonging to the Duke of Rutland. He had sent John Carleton to Cley for the purpose of 'veueng the decay of the Haven there thorow the inning (embanking) of a marsh at Saltehouse'.[5]

About the same time (1522/3) some of the Duke of Rutland's tenants in Cley had pulled down a bank 'made without leve on my maister's grounde and lettyng (i.e. impeding) the water in the Haven his old course'.[6] This had led to a bill of complaint from tenants in Blakeney, who presumably had built the bank and diverted the channels. This was the first of many similar disputes.

1547   The mariners of the Glaven also had to fight the natural processes of deposition in order to keep their channels navigable. In 1547 they made a request to the Court of Augmentations for permission to divert a channel so that the water would 'enter into suche parte of the haven as by the vyolence thereof the sands in the said haven shulde be repelled (di)mynyshed and washed into the sees agayne.'[7] They were granted permission and the channel from Stiffkey appears to have been dammed and diverted eastwards through a new cut, known as Bower Creek, into the main Glaven channel.[8]

The year 1565 saw a major change in the way that English ports were organised, with a view to increasing customs' revenue. **1565** The result was stricter control, the introduction of the Port Books and the port officials responsible for compiling them. Blakeney Haven was one of the creeks under the jurisdiction of Yarmouth, and described in the Survey of Ports and Creeks that year as consisting of three parts: 'the first is Clay, the second is Wiveton and the third is Snitterly which being served with several crekes onto the same haven…all in the syhte of the Customer of Clay within the port of half a myle.'[9] Later, in the same document, it is recorded that Barnard Base was the Deputy Customer and had held the post for the last seven years.

The same year provides the first detailed survey of the ports, allowing a comparison to be made with others in Norfolk. The survey distinguishes between the larger ships, termed 'Shippes for Island' and the smaller 'Crayers and boats of burthen' which were described as carrying herring, coal, corn and merchandise. The following table shows that, although Yarmouth had the largest fleet, Blakeney Haven had more Iceland ships and a larger fleet than either Lynn or Wells.[10]

Table 2: Survey of Ports 1565

Port	Iceland ships	Boats of Burthen	Total
Cley	9	14	23
Wiveton	1	5	6
Blakeney	4	8	12
Glaven total	*14*	*27*	*41*
Yarmouth	7	104	111
Wells	7	7	14
Lynn	5	12	17

Seven years later there was another survey of merchant ships completed by Thomas Colshill, the Surveyor of the port of **1572** London, headed: 'The number of shippes and vessels…..being in all the portes and crekes within the realme of Englande' taken from the customs' accounts. This survey did not discriminate between Iceland ships and boats of burden but instead recorded all ships of over 6 tons in size.[11]

Table 3: Port Survey 1572

Port	No. of ships over 6 tons	Tonnage of largest ship
Cley	13	60 tons
Wiveton	5	40 tons
Blakeney	16	60 tons
Glaven total	*34*	*60 tons*
Yarmouth	67	100 tons
Wells	11	50 tons
Lynn	24	100 tons

Table 3 shows a similar pattern to seven years earlier. However, these figures were not based on local knowledge, but taken from secondary customs' documents and compiled in London, so their accuracy might be questioned. Research, published on the accuracy of the Port Books, suggests that they under recorded the true extent of trade.

1573/4

The Port Books were special parchment books kept by customs officials and returned to the Exchequer each year. While the first of these books to survive for Blakeney were the coastal books for the period Michaelmas to Easter 1567/8, the first complete year for both coastal and overseas records cover the period Michaelmas to Michaelmas 1573/4.[12] These books show that the backbone of the coastal trade was the importation of coal from the north east and the exportation of grain and salted fish (brought in from Iceland). Many other commodities were handled: salt, timber, iron, wine, luxuries, cloth and household goods arrived regularly as well as saffron, flax, animal skins, peas, beeswax and butter.

The foreign trade was also important accounting, on average, for a quarter to a third of all the trade recorded in the Port Books. Ships regularly visited Iceland returning with fish, and occasionally, wool, cloth, whale meat and gyrfalcons. A variety of goods came from Holland and Flanders, including brick, iron, building stone, pitch, rope and soap. Norway and the Baltic provided iron, timber, canvas and rope. Salt (for the fish trade) and wine came from France and Spain. The major export was grain and malt, although large numbers of rabbit skins went to Danzig. Coal acted as serviceable ballast if grain and malt were scarce.[13]

Another detailed survey from 1580 shows Blakeney Haven as second only to Yarmouth and as important as Lynn. Direct comparisons with 1565 are difficult as there was little uniformity in the way that the figures

Plate 15: Tudor ships from the 1586 map.

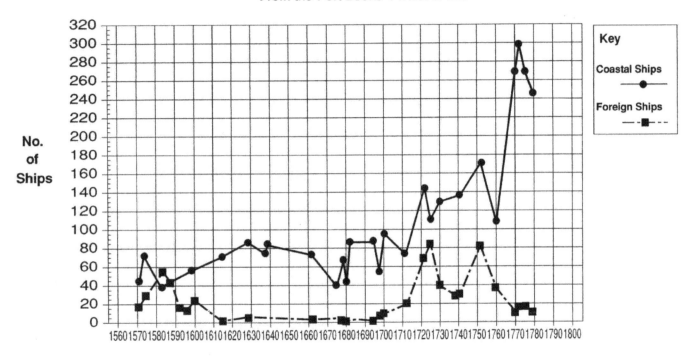

Number of Ships Cleared In and Out, Divided into Coastal and Foreign

From the Port Books P.R.O. E 190

Figure 1: Ships cleared in and out from the Blakeney Port Books.

were compiled, however, the ships do appear to be larger and the rise in importance of Wiveton is striking. Wiveton also possessed the largest ship, the *Marie Grace* (120 tons), as well as three other vessels of 100 tons. Only three larger vessels are mentioned in the same document, the *Blacke Lion* of Lynn (140 tons), the *Clementes* of Wells (160 tons) and the *Gyfte of God* of Yarmouth (200 tons). The figures in Table 4, taken from this survey show that the Haven was an important and prosperous Norfolk port.[14]

Table 4: Certificate of Maritime Resources in Norfolk 1580

Port	No. of Ships
Cley	11
Wiveton	13
Blakeney	11
Glaven Total	35
Yarmouth	61
Wells	19
Lynn	32

1586   1586 is the date of the first detailed map of the area (map 2 p. 6). It was made to accompany a dispute about which manor held the Right of Wreck—the selling of cargo or ships' materials salvaged from a wreck could be a very profitable business. Goods collected from a Scottish ship wrecked at nearby Runton recorded in the Port Books included barrels of prunes and honey, alum, licorice, aniseed, pepper and playing cards, amongst other things. The result of the dispute is not known, but it does indicate that this part of the coast was seen as valuable and worth getting involved in a costly legal case, indicating a prosperous level of trade. Other benefits of the coast are seen in the illustrations shown on the map. There is a shepherd/warrener (with what looks like a ferret on a lead, maybe after rabbits) tending a flock of sheep grazing on Blakeney Eye and just north of Morston, and others on the marshes, who appear to be cockling, or possibly collecting bait or samphire.[15]

1588   Blakeney was included in the plans to defend Britain against the Armada but emerged with little credit from the affair. As the threat of invasion loomed, Blakeney, along with Lynn, was asked to supply two ships of 60 tons minimum and a pinnace to defend their country. The mayor and aldermen of Lynn provided the *Mayeflower* of 150 tons and a 40 ton pinnace, but complained that 'we hadd conference with some of the chefest of the saide Towne of Blakeney and with some of the Townes of Claye and Wyveton w'ch be members of the same Towne of Blakeney, and we fynde that they are unwilling to be att any chardge neare the furnyshyng of a Shipp.' There was a similar unhelpful response from Wells and the men of Lynn suggested the council tried writing to Blakeney again.[16]

There were fears that the deep water inshore at Weybourne (known as Weybourne Hope) may have been an invasion site and a map 'made In hast this fyrst of May 1588' by Edmund York shows plans to build two forts at Weybourne and Blakeney as well as a wall and 'intrenchment' along the marshes at Salthouse. The possible remains of the Blakeney fort can be seen east of the river Glaven on Cley Eye. The Weybourne fort would have fallen into the sea long ago but a field name at the coast 'Sconce and No Man's Friend Furlong' on a 1704 estate map of Weybourne, would seem to indicate that it had been built, since a sconce was

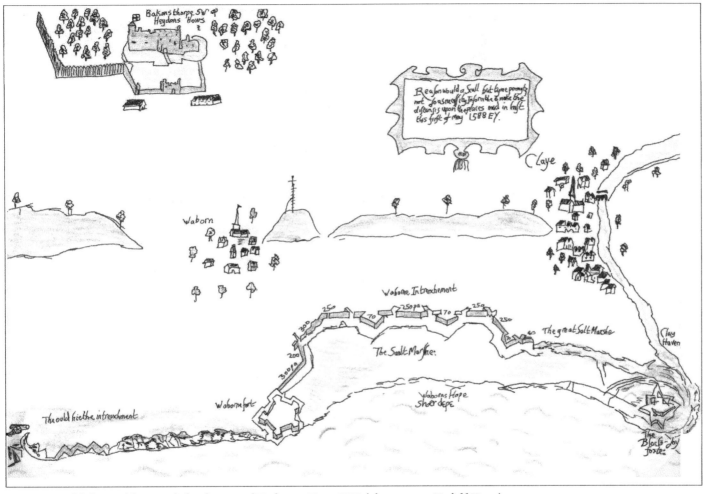

Map 7: A simplified map of the Armada fortifications of Weybourne Hope, 1588 (after a map at Hatfield House).

another name for a fort.[17]

The end of the 16th century marked the peak of the Glaven's prosperity. In 1590 two ships, the *Ambrose* and the *Laundrel* left

1590

EVIDENCE BOX 7: BLACKJOY FORT

EVIDENCE here is not easy to see and involves the use of the imagination. The relief is very subdued, but during the summer, subtle changes in the vegetation will mark out small variations in the height of the land. Standing by the road and looking northwards towards the sea, it is quite possible to see that the land to the east rises higher than the marsh to the south and the shingle to the north. This is Cley Eye (or island) which rises above 5 metres. There are a series of 'eyes' scattered through the marshes composed of glacial moraine. These were mounds of glacial material moulded under the ice sheet and left behind as islands in among the marshes when the ice sheets melted. A walk of 3½ km east along the beach will take you to what is left of the largest of them, called Gramborough Hill, rising above 10 metres. It is slowly eroding as the shingle bank moves inland with each tidal surge. An exposed un-vegetated cross section reveals the jagged, frost shattered, flints within the sand confirming its glacial origin.

According to the 1588 map (map 7 p. 37), the Armada fort was located to the west of the road, next to the channel leading to Cley, so that it would be able to guard against ships sailing up the channel. It is not at all clear on map 7. It is more of a scribbled afterthought, crammed in at the very edge of the plan. It appears to be a star shaped fort and named, Blackjoy fort.

In 1951, former Cley local historian, Magnus (Peter) Catling, made a sketch plan of what he considered were the earthwork remains of the fort (map 8 p. 39). He recalled that much of this was destroyed by the storm surge of 1953. If you are persistent enough to wade through the marshland towards the old channel, it is possible to see what looks like banks of higher land next to ditches, picked out by differing vegetation that do seem to take strange turns. Could this be the faint remains of a hurriedly constructed Armada fort?

Further Reading

Cozens-Hardy, B (1938) Norfolk Coastal Defences in 1588 in *Norfolk Archaeology* vol. 26 p. 311.

O'Neil, BH St J (1941) The fortification of Weybourne Hope in 1588 in *Norfolk Archaeology* vol. 27 p. 253.

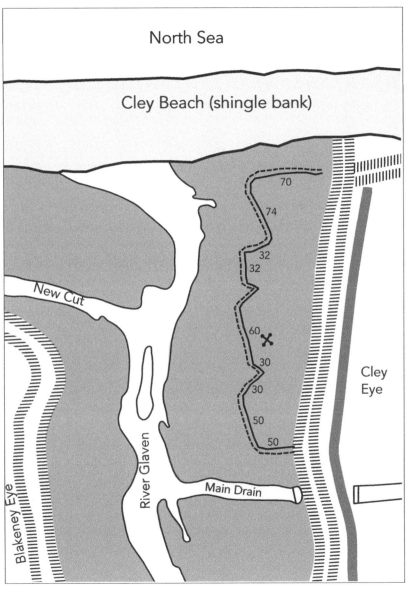

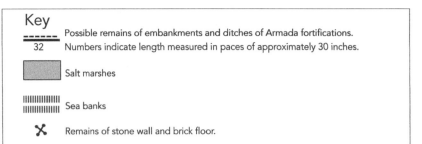

Key

------- Possible remains of embankments and ditches of Armada fortifications.

32   Numbers indicate length measured in paces of approximately 30 inches.

Salt marshes

Sea banks

✗   Remains of stone wall and brick floor.

Map 8: Sketch Plan of earthworks on Cley Eye by JJ Hooton (after M Catling).

Plate 16: Bank east of Cley Eye possibly a remnant of Blackjoy Fort.

Cley for Crete. The *Ambrose* had been in Marseilles the previous year. The Glaven's ships were keeping pace with all the ventures initiated by the larger ports and were sailing north to Iceland, south to the Mediterranean, west from Ireland and east to the Baltic. This led Neville Williams (a former Deputy Keeper of the Public Record Office) to write 'This first voyage of Benjamin Bishop and Clement Wilkinson to Crete symbolizes the vitality of the trade of the small port of Blakeney at the end of the sixteenth century. The Elizabethan spirit of enterprise was not the prerogative of the Port of London. This was not to continue into the next century. Although the actual volume of traffic increased in later centuries, the relative importance of the ports had declined. The harbours were not deep enough and the hinterland was not large enough to provide a lucrative enough market, nor was the finance available to allow ships to venture across the oceans. The 17th century would see a transition to a local port, primarily engaged in the coastal trade. Two major events would take place to hasten that decline.[18]

Notes

1   Blomefield, F *An Essay towards a Topographical History of the County of Norfolk* (cont by Parkin, C., (1805–10) VIII p. 104).

2   Carus-Wilson, EM (1967) *Medieval Merchant Venturers* London University Paperback p. 127.

3   Fraser, CM (ed) (1987) *The Accounts of the Chamberlains of Newcastle Upon Tyne 1508–1511* Newcastle, The Society of Antiquaries of Newcastle Upon Tyne.

4   Wright, J (1998) Sounds familiar…but what does it mean? in *The Glaven Historian* no.. 1 pp. 27–29 and Wright, J. (1999) Sounds familiar (Part II)…The first new cut? in *The Glaven Historian* no. 2 pp. 9–13.

5   *The Manuscripts of his Grace the Duke of Rutland* TNA: Historical Manuscripts Commission (HMC) vol. (IV) (1905) p. 263.

6   ibid., p. 263.

7   The National Archives (TNA): PRO E321 7/3 quoted in ibid., 4 pp. 27–29.

8   ibid., 4 pp. 27–29 & pp. 9–13.

9   TNA:PRO E178 Special Commission 1528 7 Eliz. I.

10   Norfolk Record Office (NRO) 523 *A Survey of the ports, creeks and landing places of Norfolk 1565* (facsimiles and transcripts of selected folios from TNA, SP12/38).

11   Green, MAE (1871) *CSP Domestic Elizabeth, Addenda 1566–79* London p. 440.

12   TNA: PRO E190 472/1; E190 473/10.

13   Hooton, JJ (1996) *The Glaven Ports* Blakeney, Blakeney History Group ch. 11 pp. 84–88 & ch. 12 pp. 89–93.

14   Smith, AH & Baker, G (eds) (1982/83) *The Papers of Nathaniel Bacon of Stiffkey vol. II* Norfolk Record Society & Centre for East Anglian Studies U.E.A. p. 143–50.

15   Hooton, JJ (1998) 1586 Map of Blakeney Haven and Port of Cley Part I in *The Glaven Historian* no. 1 and Wright, J (1999) 1586 Map of Blakeney Haven and Port of Cley Part II in *The Glaven Historian* no. 2; Frostick R (2005) A 16th Century East Anglian Surveyor, and Peter Breugel in *The Journal of the International Map Collectors' Society* no.101 p. 33; Cozens-Hardy, B *Maritime Trade of Blakeney, Norfolk 1587–90* Norfolk Record Society vol. VIII p. 28.

16   Letter to the Council dated April 12 1588 in *Defeat of the Armada* Navy Record Society quoted in Hillen, HJ (1907) *History of the Borough of King's Lynn* vol. 1 Norwich pp. 294—5.

17   Map of Weybourne, Hatfield House Library CPM11/36; also NRO MC 2443/2 A Mapp of Wayborne in Norfolk 1704.

18   Williams, N (1988) *The Maritime trade of the East Anglian ports, 1550—1590*. Oxford: Clarendon Press.p. 127, p. 131—2; Cozens-Hardy, B (1936) The Maritime Trade of the Port of Blakeney, which included Cley and Wiveton 1587 to 1590 in *Norfolk Record Society* vol. VIII p. 36.

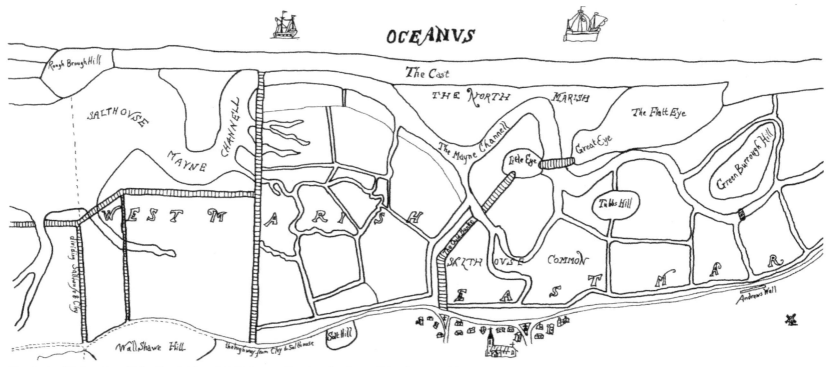

Map 9: simplified version of John Hunt's Map of 1649 showing Van Hesedunck's 'oulde bank' near Salthouse Common.

5: Seventeenth Century Decline and Stagnation
Fire, Embankments and Admirals

IF the surviving Port Book information for the 17th century is considered (see figure 1 p. 35) then the coastal trade could only be described, at best, to have remained steady. There was no growth, and this indicated a relative decline compared with ports elsewhere. The overseas trade appears to have dwindled to an occasional voyage a year. This marked a century of stagnation, if not decline. It did not start very promisingly with two events, a major fire and then the interference caused by the embanking of the marshland.

In 1612 a major fire in Cley destroyed 117 buildings, although no lives seem to have been lost. It must have consumed a substantial part of the settlement, the 'Towne' of Cley being of significant size. The 1586 map (map 2) shows 59 separate buildings in a dense cluster around Newgate Green and the church, the settlement straggling northward to beyond where the two channels meet at the present day site of the windmill. That Cley spread as far north as it does today is confirmed by the manor court books, which record that Adam Kindt owned a house 'lying under Anderton Hill'. Adam Kindt was a prominent foreign merchant living in Cley who died in 1598. The present day Anterton Hill is the higher land above the coast road looking out over the marshes and a good kilometre north of Newgate Green. Widow Newgate lost most houses (18) in the fire and since Newgate farm is to the east of the church and Newgate Green lies in front of it, perhaps this was the area most severely damaged. The fire could have speeded up the migration of the village northwards, away from the church, although Basil Cozens-Hardy, in his analysis of property descents, felt that the fire was in the northern part of the town. Although substantial damage was done, it seems likely that only a part of the settlement was destroyed, for the shipping was little affected and the town soon recovered.[1]

The same recovery did not happen to Wiveton after Sir Henry Calthorpe, the Lord of the Manor, built a bank across the Glaven valley in 1637, its line being approximately the present coast road. The purpose was to reclaim marshland. Although the Cley quays were on the seaward side of the bank, Wiveton became cut off from the sea and cargo had to be unloaded and lightered up to quays. The Cley mariners expressed concern about the silting up of the main channel due to the lack of scour. Two protests from local courts came to nothing, so the mariners petitioned the Privy Council. The petition stated that they owned: '19 other good shipps, some of 140 tons and one of 160 tons', six of which had been built at Wiveton, and that the channel north of the bank had 'already groune up and landed 2 foote at least'. Their lordships found in favour of the mariners, and the bank was ordered to be pulled down. However, the damage had been done. Two years of interrupted trade had forced merchants to look elsewhere. Wiveton never recovered and trade at Cley became predominantly coastal.[2]

1612

1637

1649   Despite the legal victory of the Cley mariners the impetus for embanking gained pace. A Dutchman, Van Hasedunck, rumoured to be living at Cley Old Hall, and who had probably been responsible for Calthorpe's bank, had been reclaiming marshland in Salthouse as early as the 1630s. Another law suit, from Lady Sydney, resulted in part of that bank being removed. However, by 1649, John Hunt's map (map 9 p. 42) of Salthouse and Kelling marshes 'as they were Imbanked & divided into Common & Severall inclosures' shows a much greater area embanked than in 1630. The lack of scour must have had a detrimental effect on the main channel for both Blakeney and Cley.[3]

1650   On 25 November 1650, Cloudesley Shovell, the most famous seaman to come from the Glaven valley, was baptised at Cockthorpe, a small village overlooking Blakeney. His father, John Shovell, owned land in Morston and was probably farming at Cockthorpe. His mother was Anne Jenkenson of Cley. His maternal great grandfather, Thomas Cloudesley, from whom he gained his Christian name, owned land in Cley. Although Cloudesley Shovell must have been acquainted with the port as a boy, it is unlikely that he sailed in Cley ships. His father died when he was 3 and his mother married John Flaxman at Gimmingham when he was eight. Although, in later life, they returned to the Glaven valley the young Cloudesley probably moved to Gimmingham.[4]

Curiously enough, the other two admirals from the area were born within 25 years of Cloudesley and were possibly distant relatives. Sir Christopher Myngs was baptised in Salthouse in 1625. His mother, Katherine Parr, came from a seafaring family who owned ships and land in Salthouse. Myngs, who was knighted in 1665 after the Battle of Lowestoft, rose to the rank of Admiral of the Red* before being killed in action at the Four Day Fight in 1666. Sir John Narborough (or Narbrough), who was knighted in 1674 and rose to the same rank, was also baptised in Cockthorpe in 1640. The naval careers of all three admirals were intertwined, with Cloudesley Shovell even marrying Narborough's widow three years after Narborough died of a fever in the West Indies.

Shovell was at sea by the age of thirteen, serving with Myngs and Narborough in the West Indies. In all likelihood, the *Centurion* was his first ship with Myngs, as captain, and Narborough as lieutenant. Shovell, after an illustrious career, which included the capture of Gibraltar, became a Member of Parliament and Admiral of the Fleet, before drowning when his ship, the *Association*, struck rocks off the Scilly Isles. Whether he ever returned to the Glaven is doubtful, but he remained close to his mother and supportive of his family. He lies buried in Westminster Abbey.[5]

1667   The Port Books were not kept during the Commonwealth period (1649–60) and there is a lack of documentary evidence for the mid-17th century. A few years after the Restoration, the fortunes of the Glaven Ports did not look healthy. In 1667, a petition to the Lord High Admiral indicated a decline in fortunes by recording that: 'by reason of the many losses the merchants of the said townes have met with they are discouraged to adventure their estates by which means the harbour is ruined.' The 22 signatories, headed by Sir Cloudesley's uncle, Cloudesley Jenkenson, requested a salary for the 'Haven man' for 'the maintenance of his boyes and Beacons.' The inadequacy of the harbour could reflect the damage done by the embanking but it may just be due to general fluctuation in trade. The Port Books would support this latter view. Table 5 shows the number of cargoes carried in a year and the

Plate 17: Sir Cloudesley Shovell by Michael Dahl c1702.

Plate 18; Sir Christopher Myngs attr. Peter Lely (Royal Museums Greenwich).

* The Navy was divided into three squadrons Red, White and Blue in order of seniority. The Admiral of the Red was second and Blue was third in precedence. The Admiral of the Fleet was first.

EVIDENCE BOX 8 : CLEY CHURCH AND CHURCHYARD

THIS magnificent church is again a testimony to the wealth that the port brought to the village. Its rebuilding started in the 14th century and after a pause, probably due to the effects of the Black Death, was completed at the start of the 15th century. Its position, quite a way south of the centre of the present village, reflects the original site of the port in the more sheltered part of the estuary, as indicated today by the triangular Newgate Green.

At the east end of the south aisle there are a couple of brasses of the wealthy shipowning family, the Symondes. The older is to John Symondes, who died in 1502, and his wives Agnes and Margaret. John was a merchant and shipowner. According to his will, he had four ships out at sea, as well as the *Jamys* which was in port. It seems to be a rather rushed will, for all of them were to be, 'disposed of by my executors'. His son, also John Symondes, and wife Agnes, whose shroud brasses are also in the south aisle behind the organ, had more organised wills.

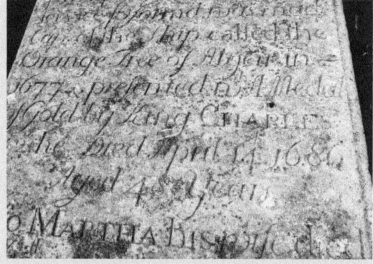

Plate 19: The top of James Greeve's table tomb near the south transept.

John the younger's will of 5 January 1508 states that he left his wife, 'the great ship whan she comys home owte of Iselond' and it was up to her if she kept or sold it. The trade to Iceland meant salt fish. The *Trynitie* was to go to his son, Rauf, when he came of age (20) and, until then, was to be managed by his executor to provide funds to pay for his schooling. His executor was to use the salt he possessed (another indication that he was involved in the salt fish trade) to make sure all his ships were equipped to go to sea this coming summer, 'to be found with tackle and victuals…at my cost'. His wife was also to inherit the *Leonard* and the *Agnes* and two of his associates, Robert Rotelsome and John Bull, were to have the *Margaret,* but were also tasked with helping his wife 'to order her ships'. This shows a wealthy merchant, who owned several ships which appeared to be involved in fishing and ,in particular, with the Iceland trade. Agnes obviously kept the ships and must have made a good job of managing them as in her will, 3 years later, she asked for her 3 ships, the *George* (presumably the great ship referred to by her husband) the *Leonard* and the *Agnes* 'to be found to sea' by her executors for the next 3 years and then the *George* and the *Leonard* were to go to her son Rauf and the *Agnes* to her daughter, Agnes, when she got married.

The mariners of the Glaven sailed to Icelandic waters for one thing, the rich fishing grounds. The boats would leave the Glaven in February or March and be away for six months. Setting up a base in Iceland, they would fish and salt their catch, before returning by August with large cargoes of salted fish. Robert Hitchcock, writing in 1580, says of the trade, 'To fishe for Codde and Lyng in Iselande the Shippes commonly must go forthe in Marche and returne loden in August'.

In the churchyard, near to the tracery of the ruined south transept window (probably the work of renowned medieval mason John Ramsay, who had worked on Norwich Cathedral), is a table tomb. It is the final resting place of James Greeve. Although now heavily weathered, it reads he was 'assistant to Sr Cloudesly Shovel in burning ye Ships in ye port of Tripoly in Barbary Jan 14th 1676 and for his good services perform'd was made Capt.of the ship called the *Orange Tree of Algier*'. In 1677, Greeve was presented with a Gold medal by Charles II. Sir Cloudesley Shovell was one of three famous Restoration admirals, along with Myngs and Narborough, who were all born near the river Glaven within 25 years of each other. They were followed into service by other Glaven seamen such as James Greeve. Sir Cloudesley's mother was Anne Jenkenson from Cley and a descendent of George Brigg, who has a fine commemorative brass in Wiveton church. Shovell was in the Mediterranean with a squadron commanded by Sir John Narborough, who had also been baptised in Cockthorpe church ten years before Sir Cloudesley, in 1640. He had taken his fellow Norfolk companion with him on a mission to subdue the Barbary pirates who were interfering with British merchant men. They were based in Tripoli where they had the protection of the Dey. Narborough had been negotiating with the Dey with little success, so Sir Cloudesley, led a daring commando style raid on the pirate ships in Tripoli harbour, managed to set fire to 4 of their ships. In Narborough's words: 'About 12 of the clock in the night, my boats resolvedly entered the Port, seized the guard-boat, boarded the ships, fired them and utterly destroyed them all; some Turks and Moors slain, the rest fled to save themselves. These four ships lay under the deep castle walls, which were all in the Port excepting a Tunis merchant ship, which I ordered should not be meddled with, so escaped firing. This action was performed in less than an hour's time without sustaining the least damage on our part'. This account was published in the *London Gazette* and made Shovell and his compatriots heroes, so James Greeve eventually returned to the Glaven a hero as well.

Further reading:

Transcripts of Cley wills—Kenneth Allen Papers NRO MC 106/5 560 x 5 Marked E.
Webb, J (1962) *Great Tooley of Ipswich* Suffolk Record Society Ipswich.
Harris, S (2017) *The Other Norfolk Admirals: Myngs, Narbrough and Shovell.* Solihull, West Midlands Helion & Company Limited.

EVIDENCE BOX 9: SALTHOUSE CHURCH

The placename of this village is self-evident. There was a house here for storing salt, made from the evaporation of sea-water at the coast. Writing in 1724, Defoe in his *Tour through the Eastern Counties* says of Cley: 'there are large salt works and very good salt made'. The first field north of the coast road at the end of the village is a depression known as the Salt Pan. The salt was in great demand for preserving the fish caught along the coast and sold to, among others, the Royal Household. The trade was of such national importance that an Act of Parliament was passed in 1357 to regulate the trade in salt fish at Blakeney's annual fair, which sold cod and ling. Salthouse was also a port. At one time a broad channel led to Salthouse from the Glaven before the landward movement of the shingle spit eventually choked it out of existence sometime around 1850 as the spit made contact with the higher land of Cley Eye. During the second half of the 16th century, Robert Howsego is recorded in the Port Books as trading with Newcastle, Lincolnshire and Kent in a ship from Salthouse. The church, like the others in the Glaven valley, was rebuilt at the end of the 15th century (between 1497 and 1503).

A leger stone can be found near the pulpit which is a memorial to 'Mary Myngs, daughter of the valiant and renowned Sir Christopher Myngs.' His mother, Katherine Parr, had married John Myngs of St Katherine's in the City of London and in 1625 their son Christopher, most likely born in the Manor House next to the church, was baptised here in 1625. Myng's was known to boast that his mother was a 'Hoyman's daughter' and therefore he had a maritime background. He went on to have a successful naval career, and was later knighted after his participation in the Battle of Lowestoft, rising to the rank of Admiral of the Red before losing his life in action during the Four Day Fight against the Dutch in 1666. Samuel Pepys, was at his funeral. He recorded in his diary that he was approached by sailors, who had been under the command of Myngs, who asked whether Pepys could find them a fire ship so that they could avenge Myngs' death. This caused Pepys to write that: 'The truth is , Sir Chr. Mings was a very stout man and a man of great parts and most excellent tongue among ordinary men...He was come into great renowne here at home, and more abroad, in the West Indys.' Myngs was also instrumental in starting the careers of the other two famous admirals of the Glaven, Narborough and Shovells, who both served under him.

Also to be admired in this church are the excellent ship graffiti scratched onto the backs of the choir stalls and rood screen that show Tudor or early Jacobean ships that would have frequented the nearby ports.

Further reading:

Fiddian, V ed. (2003) *Salthouse: The Story of a Norfolk Village* Salthouse History Group.
Harris, S (2017) *The Other Norfolk Admirals: Myngs, Narbrough and Shovell.* Solihull, West Midlands Helion & Company Limited.
Defoe, D (1724) *Tour through the Eastern Counties* republished by The East Anglian Magazine Ipswich (reprinted 1949).

Plate 20: Position of Salthouse channels on 1649 map superimposed on Salthouse marshes today. (Photo by D. Edwards. © Norfolk Historic Environment Service.)

percentage carried in ships belonging to the home ports, taken from surviving Port Books.

Table 5: Number of Cargoes per year and percentage carried in Glaven ships

Year	No. of Cargoes	Percentage carried by Glaven ships
1639	82	55%
1662	75	24%
1680	44	16%
1683	87	19%
1697	53	83%

Although there were periods of decline, the overall usage of the harbour seems to have remained stable. However, if the proportion of cargoes carried in ships belonging to Blakeney or Cley is examined, there does seem to have been a marked depression in the fortunes of the Glaven's mariners and merchants around the third quarter of the 17th century.[6]

1676　　Trade was buoyant enough for a Special Commission to set out the official limits of the port and establish where the official quays were. Both official quays, belonging to 'Mr. Burton' and 'Simon Britif', were in Cley and all other landing places were prohibited from the 'landing or discharging, ladeing or shipping of any Good.'[7]

1693　　In 1693, Captain Grenville Collins in *Great Britain's Coasting Pilot* published a detailed map of Blakeney Haven. Collins was Hydrographer to the King and was commissioned to chart the harbours around the British coast. Yarmouth and Blakeney feature in Norfolk although a note explains that, 'Wells, Burnham, Lynn and Boston I have not surveyed being hindered by the present war: but as soon as the war shall be over I intend to survey it all.'[8] It is no surprise that a minor port such as Blakeney was included, since Collins had served alongside Cloudesley Shovell in the *Sweepstakes* under the command of John Narborough on a two year expedition to the Pacific coast of South America (1669–71). He was also with Narborough and Shovell in the Mediterranean from 1677 onwards when they were sent to subdue Barbary pirates that had been harassing British shipping. He dedicated his map of Blakeney and Cley to 'Sir Clodisley Shovel', who at that time was Admiral of the Blue.[9]

The haven is shown with beacons and buoys with a ½ fathom of water on the bar at low tide and 2 ½ fathoms at the 'Pit' behind the point. The channel leading to Blakeney is very small but leads to the only area marked 'Key'. The channel to Salthouse is shown as a broad channel heading east off the one leading to Cley where a prominent landing place is shown amongst the mud banks just where the channel divides into two. This was the Common Quay, also known as the George Key as it is in front of the site of the *George Inn*, later known as the *George and Dragon* after a new frontage was added in the 19th century. There is a handsome George and dragon carved above the old entrance .[10]

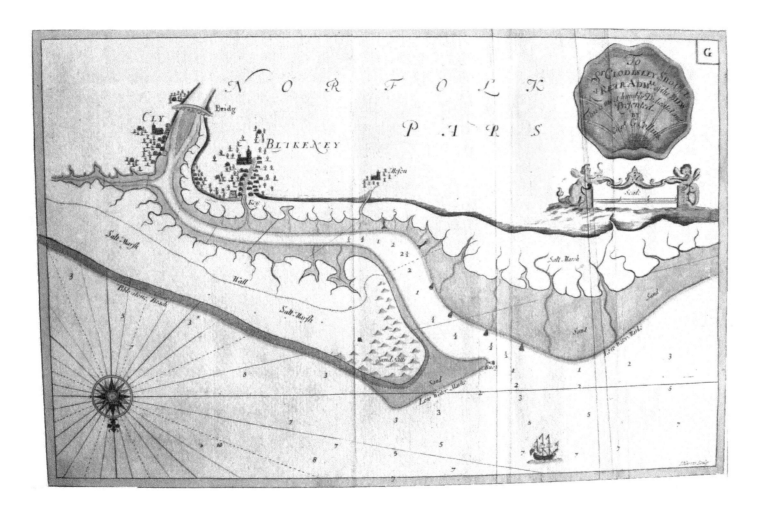

Map 10: Map of Blakeney Haven by Capt. G Collins 1693 from 'The British Coasting Pilot'. NB north is at the bottom of this map.

Notes

1   NRO MC 106 24 560 x 9 Analysis of property descents from the Cley Manor Court books; Cozens-Hardy, B The Glaven Valley *Norfolk Archaeology* vol. 33 part IV (1965) p. 510.

2   TNA: PRO Petition SP 16 vol. 424 53.

3   Anderson, V Restorations at Cley in *Norfolk Fair* (July/August 1968) p. 10; Hooton, JJ (1996) *The Glaven Ports* Blakeney, Blakeney History Group ch. 18 pp. 122–3; Cozens-Hardy, B Cley-next-the-Sea and its marshes (1926/7) *Transactions of the Norfolk & Norwich Naturalists' Society* (TNNNS) vol. 12 part 3 p. 339; Hunt, J *Map The Description of Salthouse & Kelling marishes* NRO MC 2443/1.

4   Harris, S (2017) *The Other Norfolk Admirals: Myngs, Narbrough and Shovell.* Solihull, Helion & Company Limited pp. 18–21.

5   Harris, S (2001) *Sir Cloudesley Shovell: Stuart Admiral.* Staplehurst: Spellmount pp. 1–4; Hooton, JJ ibid., 3 ch.20.

6   Petition quoted in Catling, M *History of Blakeney and its Havens* mss in Norfolk Heritage Centre pp. 138/9; Hooton, JJ ibid., 3 pp. 149–51.

7   TNA: PRO Special Commission 28 Charles II 30th October 1676.

8   Allen, K transcription from Collins Coasting Pilot NRO MC 106/8 560 x 6 pp. 6–7.

9   ibid., 5 chs 4 and 7.

10   Hooton, JJ (1996) ibid., 3 ch. 22; Collins, G (1693) *Great Britain's Coasting Pilot* National Maritime Museum 335 COL 001 20F.

6: Coastal Growth and Head Port Status
Coal in, Grain out

THe 18th century saw the start of the industrial and agricultural revolutions which led to growing towns needing to be fed and watered and to improvements in the agricultural yields, especially in Norfolk. These changes brought about an increasing agricultural surplus, particularly in grain and malting barley. These had a ready market in London, which grew steadily throughout the period. Overland transport was slow, unreliable and expensive creating an opportunity for Norfolk's ports. Trade along the coast grew rapidly as coal for industry was imported, particularly for the maltings, and grain and malt exported to London. The 18th century was the busiest in terms of coastal shipments (see Figure 1) and led to Blakeney and Cley being upgraded to the status of a Head Port.

By the opening years of the 18th century the impression is given that trade was stable and at about the same level as 100 years before. It would appear that most of this trade was in and out of Cley. The evidence comes from a Deposition in the National Archives concerning a minor dispute between the owners of a ketch, the *Martin of Lynn*, as to whether the vessel should use Blakeney, as the master was doing, or Cley, which the other owners wanted. The witnesses were questioned, among other things, about the relative merits of the ports as to which of them was 'the most convenient and commodious port for trade'.

1712

James Wells, from Sheringham, was adamant that Cley was the better port and did not know of any ships, 'that ever went to Blakeney in the said spate of 15 years past' except the *Martin*. Matthew Woods, a mariner of 30 years' experience, had not heard of any ship, excepting the *Martin*, 'resorting to the said port of Blakeney' for the last fifteen years (i.e. since 1697).[1]

Why had the thriving medieval commercial centre of Blakeney been reduced to a backwater by the beginning of the 18th century? The embanking of Blakeney marshes in the previous century may have affected the scour leading to the silting up of the channels. Also the designation, by the Commission of 1676, of only two official quays (both in Cley) and the banning of all other quays for trade, was likely to have had a serious impact on Blakeney.

The problem of official quays came to a head in 1728. An order from Lynn, that all trade must take place at a new quay belonging to Mr. Baynes, prompted an angry response from the merchants of Cley, 42 of them signing a protest letter. Not only did they see no reason why they should stop using quays, which had been operating for 'time beyond Memory of any Man', but they also criticised the new quay for being too small, not served by a public road and, 'the most remote and furthest from the Custom House'. The indication of a thriving and growing trade probably led to the quashing of the order and an expansion back to the

1728

quays at Blakeney.[2]

Four Years earlier (in 1724) Daniel Defoe had published his *Tour Through the Eastern Counties*. When describing the north

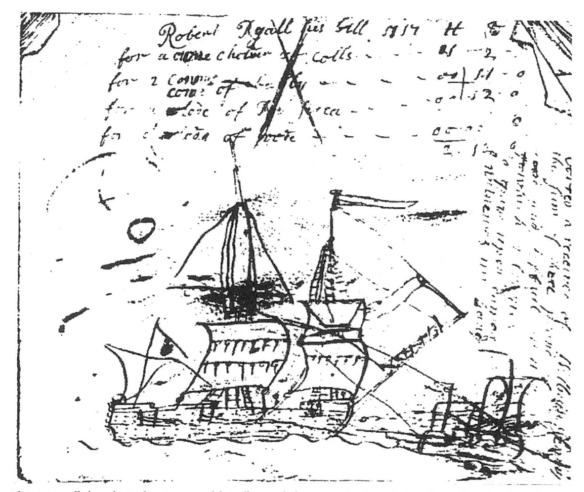

Plate 21: Doodle from the Trading Accounts of the William and Thomas 1726—1733. See The Glaven Historian (2002) no. 5 pp. 58—65. Typical of 18th century vessels that traded here. Perhaps it was meant to be the 'William and Thomas' owned by William Jennis of Weybourne.

Norfolk coast he talks of his journey 'From Cleye to go to Masham and to Wells, all towns on the coast, in each whereof there is a very considerable trade carried on with Holland for corn'. It is interesting to note that he does not mention Blakeney, again re-enforcing the impression that Cley was the more important of the two ports at this time. Of Cley he makes two further points. Firstly, that here there were, 'large salt works and very good salt made', which was sold throughout the county and sometimes sent abroad and, secondly, 'the Great Trade driven here from Holland…a Trade carryed on with much less Honesty than Advantage; especially while the clandestine Trade, or the Art of Smuggling was so much in practice'. This would keep the Customs Officers fully occupied.[3]

EVIDENCE BOX 10: CLEY CUSTOM HOUSE

BLAKENEY and Cley did not become a Head Port until 1786 but this fine Custom House (plate 22 p. 56) indicates the confidence the authorities had in the future of the coastal trade during the 18th century. Surplus produce, a result of the agricultural revolution, was being exported, largely to London and the Low Countries, with the Port Books recording a peak of over 300 vessels cleared in and out in the 1770s. Barley and malt were the main exports whilst coal was the major import, although all sorts of cargoes were shipped in small quantities. The Custom House was built about 1680 and refaced early in the 18th century. Originally the front of the building would have faced northwards, overlooking the quay. Where to put the Custom House within the haven of Blakeney had long been a problem. The Elizabethan Survey of the Ports and Creeks (1565) mentions that there were only three places within the haven of Blakeney where goods were landed, Cley, Wiveton and Snitterley. They suggested that the Blakeney Custom House be moved to Cley where all three places are 'all in the syhte of the Customer of Clay within the port of half a myle', although it is difficult to see how the Cley Customer could easily control all that was happening in Blakeney. During the 19th century the Custom House should really have been in Blakeney where there was a sub-office (according to local historian Peter Catling, at 145 High Street) as trade had declined much more rapidly at Cley. The problem was solved in May 1853 when General Order 32 from the Custom House, London, directed that 'the Customs business now transacted at Cley, be transferred to Wells' and White's Directory for 1854 states that 'the building is now occupied by the principal officer of the Coast Guard'. A sub-office remained at Blakeney, but soon control was removed from Wells to King's Lynn—a strange state of affairs since, from Elizabethan times onwards, Blakeney had always been an outport under the control of Yarmouth.

As well as admiring the architectural elegance of the Custom House, it is worth looking closely at the wooden relief over the front door (plate 23 p. 56), which gives a clue as to its former function. An officer, with cutlass drawn, followed by four excise men is seen surprising a group of smugglers who appear to be loading a packhorse from out of a two masted sailing vessel. The whole scene is local; Cley mill can be seen in the background, and the Custom House itself and, if the arrangement of doors and windows is studied carefully, it will be seen that it is the former front of the Custom House which faces the quay that is portrayed. The presence of the windmill dates the frieze to after 1820 when the mill was built. The Customs officials based here, along with the Preventive men, were kept busy throughout the 18th and 19th century dealing with what Daniel Defoe called 'the clandestine Trade, or the Art of Smuggling'.

Plate 22: Cley's Custom House.

Plate 23: Frieze over the Custom House door.

Many tall stories about smuggling exist and Cley can also lay claim to its own version of the 'Shuck' story, the demon dog, known throughout East Anglia. Peter Catling claims that 'Six foot' Arthur Bishop was the last owner of 'Shuck'—a small dark donkey with muffled hooves and a sack over its head to flatten its ears. About 15 minutes before the smugglers were to pass, 'Shuck' would be released with its own 'blind fiddler'—a boy prowling behind the hedges making horrible noises on the violin—in order to clear the way for the smugglers. It was put about that if you saw Shuck you would be dead within a week.

The very nature of the trade makes it impossible to estimate its extent, but the local papers frequently contained references to apprehending smugglers, though this must have been the tip of the iceberg. One such report will suffice here, from the *Norfolk Chronicle*, 26 February 1833: 'A desperate affray took place between the Coastguard under Lt George Howes RN and a large party of armed smugglers at Cley-next-the-Sea. The Coastguards were obliged to fire several times in self-defence. The contraband seized consisted of 127 half ankers of Brandy and between 3000 and 4000lbs. of manufactured tobacco'. However, rumours abound about the Preventive men being bribed with a keg or bale of tobacco and though they fired their guns they rarely caught or hit anybody. Likewise a keg or bale was also supposed to have been left for the shepherd on the Eye to keep his mouth shut.

Further reading:

Defoe, D (1724) *Tour through the Eastern Counties* republished by The East Anglian Magazine, Ipswich (reprinted 1949).

1730

In 1730 Horatio Walpole, the British Ambassador to France, was retiring to his country seat at Wolterton. His furniture and books had 'escap't the dangers of the sea and were arrived safely to the Haven's mouth at Cley [and] in the most unheard of manner all destroyed by the ship being sett on fire.'[4] So reported the Reverend Patrick St Clair. He went on to record that the cargo was worth £5,000 and insured to the value of £3,500 'so the loss will not be so great as people imagin'. This cargo, like the manner in which it was lost, was not commonplace. The Port Books for 1730 record a total of 170 cargoes, of which 40 involved overseas shipments. Of the rest, 56 (82% of the outward cargoes coastwise) were agricultural produce heading for London and 55 (89% of the inward cargoes) were coal from the north east ports. This pattern of 'grain out' and 'coal in' remained the basis of the Glaven's trade throughout the 18th and 19th centuries.[5]

The foreign trade, which had been so moribund during the 17th century, picked up during the first half of the 18th century. Although it fluctuated with economic conditions, up until 1760 it remained healthy, accounting for between 20 and 40% of the total trade. After that date it declined rapidly, being nearer to 5% of all the cargoes handled.[6]

1739

By 1739 there was a need to improve communications between Blakeney and Cley and a wooden bridge was built across the Glaven paid for by public subscription. This is likely to reflect the increase in maritime activity at Blakeney, especially when it is noted that it was the Collector of Customs at Cley, Patrick Eson, who undertook the task and, 'took great pains in procuring subscriptions to ye same'. The bridge was built near to where the present coast road crosses the river Glaven. This date was also the year that the Quarter Sessions recorded a payment of £20 for 'pulling down the bridge (at Wiveton) and making good the road there.' This would have been the wooden bridge over the channel on the Cley side, shown on the 1586 map, which issued onto a causeway leading to the stone bridge at Wiveton. On 30 October 1789, a high tide and gale forced the ship *Abicore* through the new bridge and halfway to Wiveton. It was soon repaired for 50 guineas. In 1799, the bridge was in a ruinous state again and repaired by subscription. The bridge features in a watercolour by JS Cotman, painted in 1818 (see plate 24 p. 59). It was presumably in use up until the bank was built across the Glaven as a result of the Enclosure Act.[7]

EVIDENCE BOX 11: ESON'S BRIDGE

THE green in front of the *George and Dragon* pub is the site of the Common Quay and it was from here that Cotman sketched the watercolour in graphite with grey and sepia washes, entitled *Blakeney Church and Wiveton Hall, north Norfolk* in 1818 as part of a series of drawings for the book, *Excursions through Norfolk*, published in two volumes in 1819. It is presently in Leeds Art Gallery. Look at the view over the concrete flood wall at the rear of the green and compare it with the Cotman watercolour. The first difference that will strike you is the absence of the present-day woodland. The tower of Blakeney Church can be found protruding above the trees, but it is very difficult to see the smaller, eastern tower, which Cotman gives prominence to. Also the windmill further down the hill has lost its sails and become a holiday home. Lower down the hill, the impressive outline of Wiveton Hall is hidden amongst the trees and there are no masts of ships lying at Blakeney quay. The mouth of the Glaven is wider than the present river and Patrick Eson's bridge can be clearly seen, approximately where the present coastal embankment is today. The embankment was constructed as a result of the 1824 Enclosure Act (a few years after this sketch) and behind which is the present coast road. The humpbacked bridge in the foreground is approached by a causeway which would have been submerged during high spring tides. On 17 February 1816, when it was impassable, five young lives were lost when they tried to cross by boat, following attendance at a chapel meeting. They had to cross a lighter, moored at Cley quay before getting into the ferry boat, which as a contemporary account puts it: 'it no sooner put off than it got foul of the rope by which the lighter was moored and instantly filled'. Though some managed to escape, five drowned in the freezing water. This bridge, though repaired, was made unnecessary by the permanent embankment, bridge and new road, where the present day A149 runs.

Further reading:

https://cotmania.org/works-of-art/43995.

Plate 24: Cotman's Blakeney Church and Wiveton Hall, showing Eson's Bridge in the foreground.

Throughout its history the Glaven valley suffered from periodic inundations from high spring tides driven onshore by northerly gales. An event referred to today as a tidal surge. In the 18th century they were known as 'Rages'. These 'Rages of the Sea' are well documented in this century by the local rectors, JW Girdlestone and Robert Thomlinson, who noted them in the Parish Registers. Flooding of the marshes, and frequently of the houses too, took place in 1735, 1741, 1744, 1749, 1767, 1779 and 1791. The most serious one in this century appears to have been in 1741 when 'a very great tide drowned all the marshes on both sides of the channel, broke down the greatest part of the marsh banks, especially the East bank which was almost wholly destroyed…There was 3 or 4 feet water in many houses and above 2 in the parsonage'. The financial damage to Richard Thomlinson, Lord of the Manor, was estimated to be £815.00.[8]

EVIDENCE BOX 12: FLOOD PLATES

THE four tide marks on the end of the old granary have always fascinated visitors. Although the oldest date is 1897, high tides have happened regularly throughout Blakeney's history when the right combination of tidal and weather conditions coincide to create storm surge events. During the 18th century they were known by the much more expressive term a 'Rage of the Sea', and there are informative notes on Rages inside the covers of the Cley parish registers. The marshes were frequently inundated ruining the grazing and any crops being grown as well as necessitating repairs to the banks. In December 1744 the sea 'drowned all Cley marshes (but not Blakeney), destroyed 20 acres of wheat growing in the marshes and did considerable damage to the banks'. Five years later, in February 1749, the sea 'made a small break in Blakeney Banks and a small part of their marshes were overflowed but none of Cley'. This was because of 'ye stoutness of the East Bank' which had been greatly enlarged in height and thickness since the year 1744. Neither parish escaped a drenching in 1769, or 1779, and the latter Rage also warranted a remark in the Blakeney parish register. Not only were the marshes drowned under at least 8 feet of water but, 'A ship lying in the Channel broke from her Mooring and beat down a great part of a House and a considerable Length of Wall upon the key'. The water also did considerable damage in Cley 'by getting into Malthouses and spoiling corn in the Granaries etc'. Perhaps the strangest event that happened to a vessel is found in Volume 3 of the Cley parish registers. Here there is a reference to a report found in the Custom House of a Rage on 25 November 1665 which not only broke the banks and flooded the marshes but 'tossed a ship out of the Sea, over the Beach into Salthouse channel which was brought to Cley to be repaired'. This unlikely occurrence undoubtedly saved the lives of the crew.

Plate 25: Flood Tide marks on the end of the old granary on Blakeney Quay.

The 1953 and 1978 flood marks were surveyed in 1998 and found to be 6.05 AOD (above Ordnance datum) and 5.50 AOD respectively. These flood levels were measurements taken by local people and did not use standardised methods.The most reliable data for the 1953 surge comes from the tide recorder at Wells, which gave 5.10 AOD. However, this is a 'still water level' reading and does not take into account the effect of wave action in addition to the increased tide levels. This would give credence to the higher mark at Blakeney, which was probably recorded using the highest 'tide mark' left, once the waters began to subside. Although it is not possible to predict when the next Rage will occur, it is inevitable that there will be one. It is also likely that they will be more severe in the 21st century if sea levels rise as predicted. Current MAFF guidelines suggest that, in East Anglia, an allowance of 6mm per annum should be made for future sea level rises.

1769

In 1769 William and Corba Cranefield produced *An exact Survey of Blakeney with part of Towns adjacent*. It is primarily a record of land holding within the parish, but it does show the harbour channels. The Cranefields were local men and mixed surveying with other occupations. Corba Cranefield was better known for his clock and watch making but was also a farmer. William ran a commercial academy with a mathematically based syllabus including surveying, gunnery and navigation. Their work showed that the channel that led from the point to Cley was termed the 'Harbour' being 264 yards wide at its western extremity. The channel to Cley was 176 yards wide, narrowing to 132 yards as it turned south round Blakeney Eye. The channel to Blakeney was narrower, 110 yards wide at its entrance and only 66 yards wide as it approached the quay. Four ships are drawn at Blakeney quay, two with two masts and two with a single mast. Another, single masted vessel and much smaller, is in the channel. Although Cley is not depicted, there are two sizeable ships in the channel, both with two masts, one approaching and one leaving Cley. The impression given is of a healthy trade at both ports.[9]

1780

This date sees the withdrawal of the Port Books for Blakeney. They had been introduced in 1565 and, although in the early years not many survived, they are the only records of trade that can be relied upon for a period of over two centuries. There has been much discussion over their accuracy but they are generally believed to be an under-estimate of the actual level of trade, certainly for the earlier period.[10] Many of the books survive for the 18th century and they show a considerable increase in trade from around a hundred cargoes a year recorded in the early years of the century to nearer three hundred cargoes by the time they were withdrawn. The last books, for 1780, show 252 coastal and 10 foreign cargoes. The exports were dominated by barley and malt being shipped to London and there was an even greater number of ships from Newcastle and Sunderland bringing in coal. Most of the East Coast ports, from Blythe in the north to Rochester in the south, were visited by the Glaven's ships.[11]

1786

The continuing growth of the coastal trade, caused by surplus grain due to the agrarian revolution and the constant demand for coal, led to Blakeney being upgraded to a Head Port in 1786. Previously it had been a creek, under the control of Yarmouth.

Notes

1   TNA: PRO Deposition E 134 11& 12 Anne Hill 33 1712.
2   *Kings Lynn Custom House Letter Book* reprinted in the Eastern Daily Press (EDP) 8 March 1924.
3   Defoe, D (1949) *Tour Through the Eastern Counties* 1724 reprinted East Anglian Magazine Ipswich p. 99.
4   Ketton-Cremer, RW (1951) *Country neighbourhood.* London: Faber and Faber. pp. 50—4.
5   TNA: PRO E190 545/9, 545/11,545/17.
6   Hooton, JJ (1996) *The Glaven Ports* Blakeney, Blakeney History Group ch. 25
7   Notes in the Cley Parish Registers NRO PD 270/3 & 4; Wright, J, (2001) The Bridges of Wiveton in *The Glaven Historian* 4 BAHS pp. 3—23.
8   ibid., vol. 3 and vol. 5.
9   NRO BL 49/1; Eden, PG (1973) Land Surveyors in Norfolk 1550—1850: Part 1 The Estate Surveyors *Norfolk Archaeology* vol. 35 pp. 474—82 and (1975) Part 2 The Surveyors of Inclosure *Norfolk Archaeology* vol. 36 pp. 119—48.
10   ibid., 6 ch. 10 pp. 78—83 and ch. 25 pp. 166—75.
11   TNA: PRO E190 585/25; 585/16, 585/9.

7: Nineteenth Century Growth and Decline
Two Acts

AT the beginning of the previous century, around 1700, trade at Cley was depressed and practically non-existent at Blakeney. Although there followed a dramatic increase in the level of trade, which undoubtedly started in Cley and led to a revival at Blakeney, it is difficult to estimate the relative contribution of the two ports. The Port Books no longer record the ships as being 'of Blakeney' or 'of Cley', which in previous centuries indicated the dominant port from which they traded. Circumstantial evidence has to be relied upon to piece together the fluctuating fortunes of the two settlements. The trading accounts of the *William and Thomas* from 1726 to 1733 throw some light on this question (see plate 21). She was owned by William Jennis of Weybourne and was registered at Blakeney but traded largely from Cley. Of the 31 voyages recorded, all but two were from Cley. However, much of the cargo had to be lightered up to the quay before the vessel was light enough to approach the quay and discharge the rest of her cargo. This was an expensive business and the profits were not great, in fact the last six voyages ended in losses.[1] Other indications of trade at this time can be found in the Cley parish registers, where the rector, Robert Thomlinson, recorded the number of parishioners and the following notes:

> 1789 422 souls. NB at this time the trade of the town declined very much—many of the Principals being dead—people went to Blakeney etc.

> 1791 I believe we are as full of inhabitants as in the year 1777 [when there were 587] Trade being very brisk and two merchants in the town.

> 1801 547 souls The Trade of the town has increased very much within these last two years—Mr Coleby, a quaker, buys and ships a considerable quantity of Corn—which finds great employment for the poor.

This probably only reflected temporary fluctuations in trade and it is possible that Mr Charles Coleby used lighters to transfer his corn from Cley into Blakeney ships. The lighters held 45 tons of cargo and would be pushed the 3 miles from the quay to the Pit by three men, one on the tiller and the other two either side of the ship with quanting poles, which would be dug into the channel. As they walked on the spot the lighter passed underneath them. As the stern of the lighter approached, they would lift their poles and walk back to the bow and repeat the process. The round trip, including loading or discharging the cargo, took about 14 hours. This would earn the men two shillings. An anonymous and roughly drawn pilot chart exists for this period (c1800). It is titled *A Chart of the Harbour of Blakeney*, a term which usually included Cley. Although a channel is shown leading in the direction of Cley, only Blakeney quay is shown on the map and the written instructions and depths also only refer to Blakeney.[2]

1803   This year saw a report on the north Norfolk coast by Major Alexander Bryce, Commanding Engineer Eastern District. Fearing invasion from Napoleon, he assessed such a possibility in Norfolk. Bryce stated of Blakeney and Cley harbour that it was, 'the best on this part of the coast. There is 20 feet water on the bar at high water. Since it has become well known it is much used by coasting vessels for shelter. The large vessels lie in what is called the PIT, and only those of small draught in general go to CLEY or BLAKENEY WHARFS'. The contemporary pilot chart, previously mentioned, stated there was 26 feet on spring tides and that the Harbour Master always hoisted a flag on the church steeple when the tide was right for entry. Seven to nine feet at low water was shown for the Pit, the name for the area of deeper water behind the point. Within 15 years, an Act of Parliament would resurrect fortunes at Blakeney while another Enclosure Act in 1821 would prove detrimental to Cley.[3]

Plate 26: Lighters at Cley quay c.1896.

1817   Whether the absence of Cley from the pilot chart marks a significant decline in its fortunes or not, it is evident that, by 1817, Blakeney was in the ascendant. This date marks the passing of an Act of Parliament for 'Improving the Harbour of Blakeney within the Port of Blakeney and Cley in the County of Norfolk.' This Act created the Blakeney Harbour Company and gave them the power to construct a new cut straightening the old winding channel in order to improve the scour of the tide and reduce silting. The new cut was designed to allow vessels of up to 150 tons to reach the quay at Blakeney. The Directors were given powers to license pilots, appoint a harbour master, keep buoys, beacons and mooring chains in good repair and levy dues on ships and cargoes. This Act gave Blakeney a new lease of life and ensured its dominance over Cley for the rest of the century.[4]

1821–4   No sooner had one Act of Parliament stimulated trade at Blakeney than another sealed the fate of Cley. The Wiveton and Cley Embankment Act was passed in 1821 with the intention of building a bank across the Glaven more or less where Lord Calthorpe's ancestors had tried to build one in the 17th century, to enclose the tidal lands of the valley up to Glandford. This time, although it threatened the port, there seemed little serious opposition. In 1822, some of the principal proprietors met the Commissioners and had the works halted whilst a second opinion was obtained. This time, the eminent engineer, Thomas Telford was instructed to re-survey the works with the remit 'to take into consideration the effect which it will have upon the harbour of Cley, any

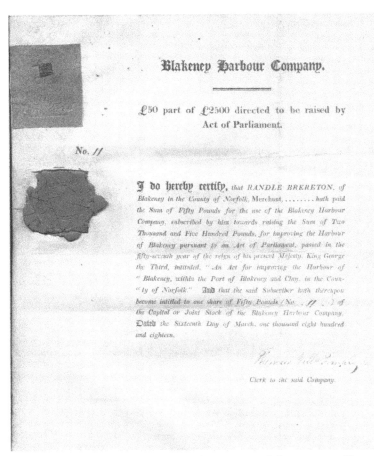

Plate 27: Share No 11 of the Blakeney Harbour Company belonging to Randle Brereton.

injury to which must be avoided'. Telford advised them that the present plan would prove injurious to the port and proposed a compromise plan that would allow tidal waters to reach Glandford along a narrow channel. This would only involve a loss of 25 acres from the proposed reclamation of the flood plain. Two other plans were also considered, but the extra costs were obviously not acceptable and on 10 April 1823 the decision was taken to ignore Telford's advice and proceed with the original plan. The bank was completed in 1824 with disastrous effects on Cley.[5]

A detailed and accurate plan of the harbour was executed by Mr Henry R Palmer in 1835. Palmer, a Fellow of the Royal Society, specialised in the surveying for roads, railways, navigation and drainage. He collaborated with Thomas Telford, but it is not clear why the survey was undertaken. His map included channel depths, which illustrate the decline of Cley. The depth of high water spring tides at Cley quay was given as six feet, compared with ten feet at Blakeney quay. He also showed the remains of the channel that led to Salthouse Broad between the shingle bank and Cley Eye 'now shut up by the shingle'. The landward movement of the spit had deprived the channel of scour from the waters that used to ebb from the 540 acres of Salthouse Broad.[6]

Palmer's map indicated that there was seven to ten feet at low water in the Pit, a deeper section of the main channel to the south of Blakeney Point. The Pit was used by larger vessels that unloaded their cargoes into lighters and was also a useful refuge for sailing vessels needing a sheltered anchorage when caught in a northerly gale. During the first

1835

half of the 19th century there was a steady, if not flourishing, coastal trade using ships of 40 to 80 tons. The goods carried showed little change from previous centuries. As well as coal from the north east and general goods and groceries from London, the importation of linseed and rape cakes became more important, as well as oats, which arrived in small but regular quantities. The major change in exports was that malt was now a rarity. The two ships called *Hull Packet* were trading regularly between Blakeney and Hull, and sometimes Goole, whereas the *Blakeney Packet*, along with other vessels, traded regularly with London. Herrings also went regularly to Boston in the winter months. The barley left as grain, along with flour, wool and potatoes. The foreign trade was minimal and in decline. Occasional cargoes of grain left and timber and oil cakes came in return. Many of the colliers left in ballast and imports continued to be more important than exports.[7]

1839   It is important to note that during the first half of this century, several ship owners invested in larger ships, the majority of which never visited the Glaven. Two typical examples are the *Ann* and the *Enterprise*. The *Ann of Clay* was a brig of 125 tons built at Peterhead in 1830 and re-registered at Cley in 1839. Her new owners were Thomas Beckwith, a clerk from Cley who owned 32 shares; Marjorie Moore, a widow from Cley (16 shares); John Copeman, a butcher from Cley (8 shares) and Phoebe Digby, the wife of a Cley shoemaker, also with 8 shares. The *Ann* probably never entered Blakeney and traded mainly between London and Hamburg. Her master, Francis Plumb, was a Blakeney man, who bought Phoebe Digby's shares in 1842. Two years later he sold them to Robert Mann and bought the *Susannah of Cley* (19 tons), to concentrate on fishing. In 1847 the *Ann* was sold again and re-registered at Workington.[8]

The *Enterprise* was a schooner, built locally at Morston and registered at Cley on 23 May 1842. She was 106 tons, although she was re-measured a month later, at 126 tons. Eleven separate investors owned shares coming mainly from Blakeney but also Salthouse, Stiffkey and Edgefield. Ownership regularly changed hands until 1846 when she was sold to WJJ Bolding of Weybourne and William Monement of King's Lynn. Bolding was a descendant of William Jennis, whose vessel, the *William and Thomas*, had traded from Blakeney in the 1730s. William Monement was a cork merchant in Lynn who was also Bolding's brother-in-law. The next year she was re-registered in Lynn and spent most of her time in the cork trade between Lynn, Newcastle and Spain.[9]

1846   The full extent of the decline of Cley was recorded by Joseph Hume, MP, in his report to the government for the Tidal Harbours Commission of 1846. Hume was highly critical of the 1821 enclosure, concluding that 'a public harbour has been almost destroyed by the encroachment on its tidal lands' and recommended that 'no Lord of the Manor should have the power of interfering with the course of tidal waters, thereby to do injustice to a public harbour'.

The evidence was fairly conclusive. The Harbour Master, William Penton, stated that in 1790 there was 8 to 9 feet of water at Cley and that this had now reduced to 5 feet. John Starling, a shipowner, went further stating that there was 13 feet of water at the site of the embankment during ordinary tides whereas it had now dropped to between 5 and 7 feet. Howard Ramm said the channel used to be 3 times as wide and William Cooke remembered that his schooner, the *Bell*, 54 feet in length, used to be

Plate 28: The Ann of Clay painting by J Hansen at Hamburg 1841. Master Capt. Francis Plumb.

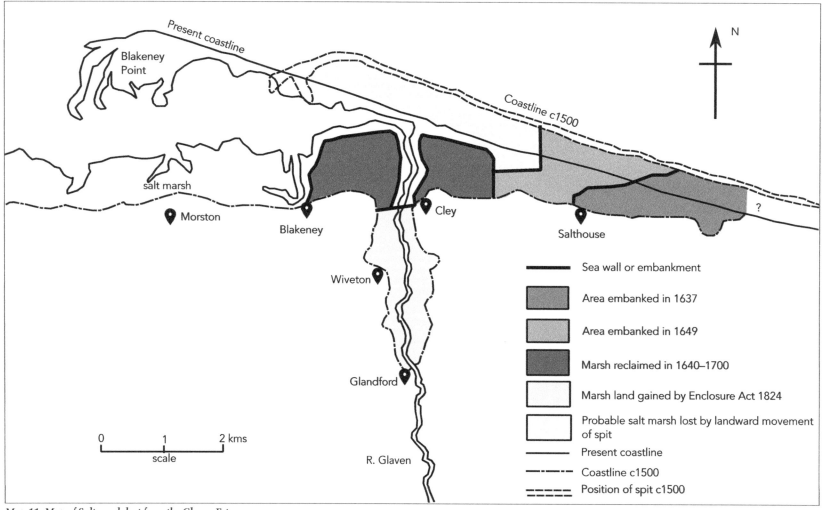

Map 11: Map of Saltmarsh lost from the Glaven Estuary.

able to be swung round at the quay. The damage was not just confined to Cley since the waters from the Glaven issued into the common channel which the Blakeney ships had to use. James Spooner, a pilot for 21 years, gave evidence that there used to be 17 to 19 feet of water at high tides over the bar at the harbour entrance, and that by 1845, this had dropped to 13 or 14 feet. Another pilot, Richard Mays, added that the deep water anchorage of the Pit had silted up so much that it was hardly deep enough for four vessels to anchor in, the depth having reduced by 8 feet, whereas he remembered as many as 140 vessels taking refuge there in the face of a north westerly gale. Only one general merchant was still left in Cley and house property had declined in value by 33% and granaries upwards of 50%. After this time very few vessels came to Cley quay and the cargoes, being lightered up, were also in decline.[10]

Trade at Blakeney, although in decline, did manage to struggle on into the next century. However, the reduced level of trade meant that Blakeney and Cley could no longer maintain their status as a head port with their own Custom House. On 31 May 1853 orders arrived from the Customs House in London to direct that 'the Customs business now transacted at Clay, be transferred to Wells, which will there upon become the head port of the District'. The same fate befell Wells. In 1880, when both Wells and Blakeney fell under the jurisdiction of Lynn, the new head port, although a sub-office remained at Blakeney for the rest of the century.[11]

1853

1859–82

At last some reliable figures can be used to indicate the level of trade and the extent of the decline in the second half of the 19th century, because an account book for the Blakeney Harbour Company has survived. Despite the natural fluctuations from year to year the graph (figure 2) indicates a steady and irreversible decline.

The highest number of cargoes in and out from the port recorded in the book (228) is in the first year and this drops to 142 by the end of the period—a decline of 37%. The figures for total usage of the harbour are sometimes higher because they include dues paid by ships using the port for refuge, but not loading or discharging any goods. When the numbers of cargoes in and out exceeds the total usage, this is because the same vessel was counted twice if it entered and left with a cargo. The usage of the harbour fell during the period from 239 to 112, a drop of 53%, with a sudden drop in the final year. The fact that the number of cargoes was larger than the harbour usage would indicate that the

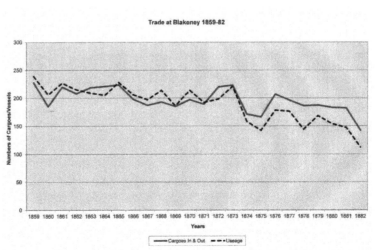

Figure 2: Trade at Blakeney 1859–1882 from the Blakeney Harbour Account Book.

trade was being handled by fewer ships and that the use of the port for refuge had declined. The number of foreign vessels using the harbour was at its most nine (1862) but dwindled to two or three with none entering in the final three years (1880–82).[12]

1870s

Despite the future looking bleak for the port, during the middle of the century, many of the shipowners were buying large ships, which were trading with Europe and the rest of the globe from other ports, often with local men as masters or crew. A good example of the enterprise shown is that of William Allen who was born in Cley in 1841. He had tried a career at sea and, by 1853, he was Mate of the *William IV*, a 63 ton schooner, built at Wells and owned locally in Cley. The maritime life did not suit William and he became the proprietor of the Weybourne post office, which was also a grocers and drapers, shortly after marrying Mary Pigot, a Weybourne girl, who had been working there in her uncle's shop. He had greater ambitions and bought his first ship, the *Parthenia*, from the local village squire, WJJ Bolding. By 1872, he managed and jointly owned 8 ships ranging in size from 167 to 318 tons. They were too large to use the local harbour and sailed from the larger ports, often to Europe, but he also had dealings with Australia, West Indies and South Africa. His cousin and brother-in-law were masters in two of his vessels. He also set up the Weybourne and Blakeney Insurance Association to insure his ships and the ships of others at Blakeney and Cley. After initial success, a series of losses from 1873 to 1881 left him with only one ship, which he sold in 1882. He went back to being a farm bailiff for the rest of his career. He typified the enterprise and scope of the local businessmen who continued to provide employment for many local men in ships sailing the globe.[13]

1862

In 1862 Blakeney received its first RNLI lifeboat, the *Brightwell*, donated by Miss Brightwell of Norwich. It was found to be too small and was replaced by a larger boat, also called the *Brightwell*, from the same donor. This was not the first lifeboat at Blakeney, since the Norfolk Association for Saving the Lives of Shipwrecked Mariners (founded in 1823) had built a lifeboat house on the Point and supplied a boat, the *Lewes Heurtwaller*, around about 1825. Little is known about this boat, but by the 1850s the Norfolk Association lifeboats were in a poor state and their administration was handed over to the RNLI in 1858. Four years later Blakeney received the *Brightwell*. Three subsequent boats were stationed at Blakeney,

Plate 29: Sail plan of the Barque 'Comus'. At 366 tons, this was the largest ships owned by William Allen.

the *Hettie* (1873–91), the *Zaccheus Burroughes* (1891–1908) and the *Caroline* (1908–35), whose combined efforts saved a total of 101 lives before the station was finally closed in 1935 (see evidence boxes 13 and 14 for more detail).[14]

EVIDENCE BOX 13: BLAKENEY CHURCHYARD
(See also Evidence Box 14)

AN examination of some of the gravestone inscriptions in the churchyard gives an indication of the importance of the port to the inhabitants of Blakeney, especially during the 19th century. Here the range of trades connected to the sea are represented: Master mariners (George Thompson), fishermen (Michael Loads), pilots (John Johnson) a Tide Surveyor (John Boyles) and Harbour Masters (Thomas Dew). There are also the grander monuments to some of the Merchants and Shipowners who provided the cargoes for the ships, such as the Breretons' vault and the Temples' obelisk at the end of the south aisle. Then, of course, there are the drownings from shipwrecks and those trying to save people in peril. Most of the Norfolk coastal villages have stories of dreadful disasters from time to time and Blakeney was no exception. In 1861, an attempt to go to the rescue of a barque, the *Favourite* of Banff, ended in disaster and resulted in Blakeney getting its own RNLI lifeboat. The *Favourite* of Banff was driven on shore at the Blakeney West Sands with a cargo of coal from Hartlepool to Torre del Mar. Eight brave Blakeney mariners took a boat out on Saturday morning (9 February 1861) at about 9.30 to attempt to rescue the crew of the *Favourite*. After crossing the bar, they met a heavy sea and a wave 'caught her on the quarter and hove her completely end over end' and most of the crew were trapped under the boat. Only 3 of the bodies were picked up and the whole crew perished. The gravestone of John Johnson, who had been a pilot for 18 years, records his death (aged 59) along with 7 others including his two brothers and a cousin. Michael Massingham, aged 56, whose stone records that his body was not washed ashore and found until three months later (13 May) was another who drowned in this accident. The body of John Easter's, aged 39, was not washed ashore until the November of that year. His stone had the couplet 'I with seven others went, Our fellow men to save, A heavy sea upset our boat, We met a watery grave'. Another boat set out and managed to rescue the crew of the *Favourite*, which soon became a total wreck.

Four other stones, David Thomas, Thomas Loads, Thomas Wisker Bowles and Thomas Loads all drowned at Mogadore (now known as

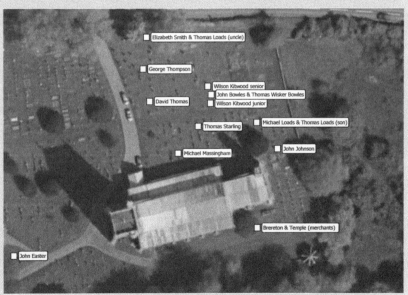

Map 12: *Blakeney Churchyard with location of selected gravestones. (Microsoft product screen shot reprinted with permission from Microsoft Corporation.)*

Essaouira, Morocco). They were in the brig *Mignonette* which was anchored off the coast and had almost finished loading her cargo. She was sunk by a tropical storm that created havoc all the way up the coast. Thomas Loads, whose body was never recovered, is mentioned twice on separate family stones. He was added to his father's stone, who had died 3 years earlier, and was included as the uncle on his niece's stone, Elizabeth Smith. The *Mignonette* was owned by Charles Temple amongst others and at 182 tons was too large to have traded from Blakeney.

Wilson Kitwood was the master of the *Hull Packet*. He was an experienced seaman and according to the gravestone, '17 years in the service of Mrs Temple'. However, a gale on 19 December 1830 led to the main boom breaking and unfortunately knocking him overboard near the floating light, about 20 miles out to sea off Blakeney. His body was eventually found in a creek on 8 September 1831. The body was in a high state of decomposition. The *Norfolk Chronicle* (10 September 1831) reported: 'he was instantly recognised by his trousers; his watch was also safe with his name on it'. The stone informs us that

I with seven others went our fellow men to save A heavy sea upset our boat we met a watery grave

Plate 30: The 1861 Lifeboat disaster by Mick Bensley

this unlikely accident led to a widow and four children being fatherless. Strangely enough, in the row behind this grave, there is a lichen encrusted stone to his son, also Wilson Kitwood, who was only 17 when he 'drowned from the brig *Equity* in the River Thames'. The *Equity* was a 116 ton brigantine built at Scarborough in 1802 and owned by the Brereton family. The only other vessel mentioned on a gravestone is the smack *Lively*, where Thomas Starling had been accidently drowned. It is a fairly worn stone in the row to the west of Wilson Kitwood. The grander obelisk and table tombs of the merchants and shipowners, the Breretons and Temples, are at the end of the south aisle.

Further reading:

Bensley, M (2006) *The rescues of the Wells & Blakeney Lifeboats* Bengunn.
Wright, J (2000) The Blakeney Disaster of 1861 in *The Glaven Historian* no. 3 p. 50.
Wright, J (2020) The Blakeney Lifeboat Station in *The Glaven Historian* no. 17 p. 48.
Gresham, S (2019) *The Blakeney Disaster 1861* Blakeney Harbour Association.
Peake, P (2004) The Highs and Lows of Living in Blakeney: Some thoughts on Mariners and their Memorials in *The Glaven Historian* no. 7 p. 60.

EVIDENCE BOX 14: BLAKENEY CHURCH INTERIOR
(See also Evidence Box 13)

BLAKENEY is another church rebuilt with maritime wealth in the 15th century. With an Early English chancel, its roof was raised and some windows replaced during this period. It was heavily restored in the late 19th century.

Apart from its dedication to St. Nicholas, the patron saint of fishermen and sailors, the three lifeboat service boards in the north aisle are the major maritime connection.

Blakeney's beachmen or companies would render rescue and salvaging services like others along the Norfolk coast, but it wasn't until the formation of the "Norfolk Association for Saving the Lives of Shipwrecked Mariners", in 1823, that Blakeney received its first true lifeboat. Little was known about this boat apart from the fact that she was probably called the *Lewes Heurtwaller*. She was kept in the Old Lifeboat House on the Point. By the 1850s, most of the boats affiliated to the Norfolk Association were in a poor state of repair. So, on 9 February 1861, it was just 'a boat' that left the harbour, with a crew of eight, to go to the aid of the *Favourite* of Banff, ashore on Blakeney West Sands. This boat was hit by heavy seas and capsized being turned 'end over end'. None of the crew survived. In a letter from

Plate 32: George Thompson, captain of the paddle tug 'Gem' rescuing William Hook, coxswain of the capsized lifeboat, 'Brightwell' after the attempt to aid the 'Faith' in May 1863 by Mick Bensley.

the Blakeney Rector to the *Norfolk Chronicle* appealing for donations to a relief fund, the men were described as: 'all married and most had families... All but one of the widows are left penniless, and one of the children has been a helpless cripple for many years. The late severe winter following on an unprecedentedly bad oyster fishing season, having long since exhausted all their hard earned gains'. It was in the year following this disaster that Blakeney received its first RNLI boat, the *Brightwell*, on 5 July 1862, at a cost of £180 pounds. On 19 May 1863 she set out to save the brig *Faith* of Rochelle, wrecked on the West Sands. The lifeboat capsized, though fortunately, no lives were lost. Coxswain William Hook and crew member John Bond were both rescued by George Thompson, the captain of the paddle tug *Gem*. He was bravely lowered over the side of the tug and managed to haul the two to safety from out of the sea. 'Lifeboat capsized. Not considered large enough for the locality' was all that the lifeboat men recorded. (Thompson is also buried in the churchyard.) She was replaced later in 1863 by a larger vessel with 12 oars, twice the number of her predecessor, and also named the *Brightwell*.

The second *Brightwell* lifeboat, also a gift from Miss Brightwell of Norwich, was in service some 12 years, being launched 12 times and saving 53 lives from the ships listed on the service board. She had a particularly successful time during the tremendous gales of October 1869. On 19 October she set off to the West Sands where the large brig the *John and Mary* of Shields (262 tons) was flying a signal of distress. The *Brightwell* managed to take off 8 men and a boy who were successfully landed at Blakeney. The following day, at daylight, another brig was seen lying on her beam ends just west of the harbour entrance. When the *Brightwell* got to her, they found her a total wreck and about to go to pieces. The crew of 6 men were exhausted clinging to the rigging and both her boats had been washed overboard. With some difficulty, the lifeboat managed to rescue them all. She was the *Ravensworth* of Hartlepool (177 tons) travelling home from Wyburg with a cargo of timber.

Plate: 33: The second 'Brightwell' lifeboat taking the crew from the brig 'Ravensworth' October 1869, a painting by Mick Bensley.

The subsequent lifeboats can be seen on the other board, being the *Hettie*, the *Zaccheus Burroughes* and the *Caroline*. This last boat was withdrawn when the station was closed in 1935. The improvement in speed of the newly motorised boats meant that adjoining stations at Wells, Sheringham and Cromer could patrol larger areas. They were also easier and faster to launch than the Blakeney boat. The growth of sand dunes and salt marsh had rendered the lifeboat house on the Point redundant. Since 1921, the lifeboat had been moored in the Pit and the old lifeboat house was given to the National Trust.

Next to the service boards is a fine model of the third Blakeney lifeboat, the *Hettie*, which served Blakeney from 1873 to 1891. She was the gift from a wealthy Bradford merchant, George Firth. The model was gifted to Blakeney by one of his descendants. She was launched four times. On 9 April 1875, she went to assist the Steam Tug *Vixen* of North Shields but her services were not required. On 21 February 1877 she went to assist the ketch *Aid* of Hull and saved the crew of 4. On 10 April 1878 she was launched to help an unknown vessel, but again her services were not required. Finally, on 25 November 1885, she went to help *HMS Beaver*. She remained with the vessel during the night and on the following morning landed her crew of 8. She had saved 12 lives during her 18 years of service, being replaced in 1891 by the *Zaccheus Burroughes*.

Plate 34: The 'Hettie' on call to the ketch 'Aid' February 1877, a painting by Mick Bensley

Further reading:

Bensley, M (2006) *The rescues of the Wells & Blakeney Lifeboats* Bengunn.
Wright, J (2000) The Blakeney Disaster of 1861 in *The Glaven Historian* no. 3 p. 50.
Peake, P (2004) The Highs and Lows of Living in Blakeney: Some thoughts on Mariners and their Memorials in *The Glaven Historian* no. 7 p. 60.
Gresham, S (2019) *The Blakeney Disaster 1861* Blakeney Harbour Association.

Although the gradual silting up of the channels continued to cause problems to shipping, it was the arrival of the railways in Norfolk which finally brought an end to the port. The bulk of the trade depended on the importation of coal, timber and oil cake, and the exportation of grain and flour; all of these commodities could be transported more quickly, cheaply and reliably by rail. A line reached Melton Constable in 1875 and, in 1884, connected Holt, only four miles from Blakeney, to the national rail network.

1882–4

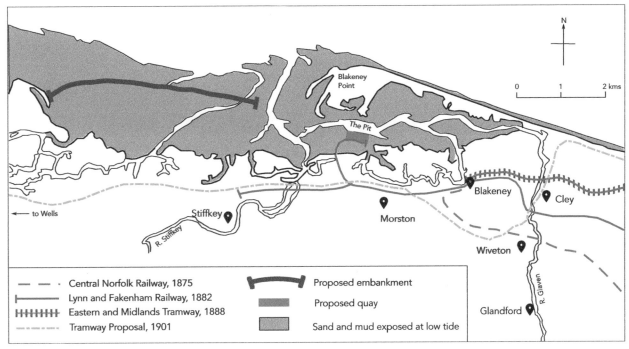

Map 13: Map of proposed railways never built.

Legend:
- – – – Central Norfolk Railway, 1875
- ├──── Lynn and Fakenham Railway, 1882
- ┼┼┼┼┼┼ Eastern and Midlands Tramway, 1888
- ·–·–· Tramway Proposal, 1901
- Proposed embankment
- Proposed quay
- Sand and mud exposed at low tide

Railways often stimulated trade to the benefit of both land and sea transport. The Lynn and Fakenham Railway had ambitious plans for Blakeney, outlined in their Railway Act of 1882. A branch line from Holt was proposed approaching the Glaven from the east, passing through Cley north of the church, crossing the river and along the marshes to Blakeney quay. It would then continue eastwards to terminate at Stiffkey. A branch line would leave the railway west of Morston and run out over the marshes on an embankment and end at a new quay, 200 yards long, to be built alongside the deeper water of the Pit. Neither had the problem of silting been overlooked. Their solution was to build an embankment from Lodge Marsh, in the neighbouring parish of Warham St Mary, three miles across the marshes to end 1,200 yards to the west of the lifeboat house on the Point. This would divert the scour from the marshes through a narrow gap either side of the channel from the Pit to the sea. Although some preliminary engineering work was undertaken, the plan was dropped and finally abandoned by another Act of Parliament in 1888. By this time the Lynn and Fakenham Railway had been amalgamated, with other companies, to become the Eastern and Midland Railway.[15]

1897

On 29 and 30 November 1897 there was a tidal surge that caused extensive flooding of the marshes in Salthouse, Cley and Blakeney. A contemporary account by Mr. Dutt recorded that:

'mighty waves coursed inland, filling the dykes and flooding the marshes…..To such a height did the water rise that the waves in some cases broke against the upper storeys of the houses, flowed out of the back doors and destroyed the buildings and garden produce in the rear. Furniture was washed out of houses and fowls were drowned by the hundred, and several villagers had to be taken out of their bedroom windows by boats and barely escaped with their lives.'[16]

The water stood in the Glaven valley for over a week and the mussel beds were ruined. Luckily no lives were lost. At sea, the *John Lee*, one of the dwindling fleet of ships still trading, had left Blakeney with a cargo of wheat for Sunderland and went down with all hands on the Woolpack Sands. This was a tragic incident. On the previous day, the *John Lee* had gone ashore and, at low tide, the crew disembarked and could have walked ashore. As the tide came in, they returned to the ship and, as the gale force waves were hitting the ship broadside on, the seams leaked. The cargo of wheat swelled and burst the hull leading to the loss of the ship and all her crew.[17]

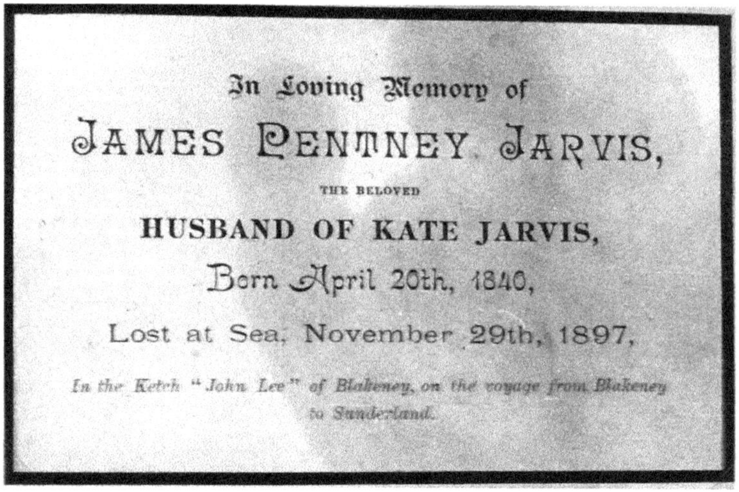

In Loving Memory of
JAMES PENTNEY JARVIS,
THE BELOVED
HUSBAND OF KATE JARVIS,
Born April 20th, 1840,
Lost at Sea, November 29th, 1897,
In the Ketch "John Lee" of Blakeney, on the voyage from Blakeney to Sunderland.

1900

The decline by 1900 was irreversible. While the Norfolk Directories were able to report that in 1888, 'there arrived at

Plate 35: Memorial card for James Jarvis lost from the 'John Lee'.

EVIDENCE BOX 15: MARINERS' HILL

A fine view of the harbour and Blakeney Point can be seen from the top of Mariners' Hill in the centre of this photograph (plate 36), although the white fencing has long since disappeared. Known at various times as Tavern Hill and Guildhall Hill, this viewpoint was used as a lookout for ships approaching the harbour. When earth was removed from one side of the Guildhall it revealed four mullioned windows which would suggest that the hill had been artificially raised after the building of the Guildhall in the 14th century. In an article about the restoration of the Guildhall in the *Eastern Daily Press* (1 May 1959), it states that 'One local story says that Mariners' Hill is made of silt dredged from the channel and dumped there by horse and cart'. Another legend has it that it contains a secret tunnel leading to the Carmelite Friary, which stood in the area to the east now occupied by Friary farm. It is down this tunnel that the blind fiddler and his cat, which appear on the village sign, are supposed to have disappeared. People on the surface followed the sound of the fiddle in an attempt to trace its route. The fiddler was never seen again. Rumours of hidden tunnels are commonplace, but when a hole appeared in the *White Horse Hotel* car park in 1976, it did reveal a brick lined tunnel coming from a chamber choked with rubble. The area of water on the left of the photograph is the oyster and mussel leys. These were filled in the 1920s with rubble from the demolition of the *Crown and Anchor* that made way for the *Blakeney Hotel*. The window, shown between the masts of the *New Walter and Ann*, allowed Page and Turner's employees a good view of the approach of their ships from the comfort of their office. The remains of the *Newcastle Packet*, being broken up on the Carnser, can be seen in the foreground, which dates the photograph to 1889.

Plate 36: Mariners' Hill c1889.

Another *Eastern Daily Press* article entitled, "Mariners' Hill, Blakeney" (31 January 1900), reported on concerns that Lord Calthorpe was, 'using same sand from the foot of this hill and some rubble from the ruins of old granaries and warehouses pulled down some years ago, to raise the roadway' to protect his marshland from flooding. The article went on to assure old sailors that the work would not reduce the height of the hill or endanger its stability. To give added reassurance they quoted from the Enclosure Act which granted the hill to Lord Calthorpe

Plate 37: Blakeney village sign with the legend of the blind fiddler and the tunnel opening.

only 'provided that it shall be lawful for all persons at all times hereafter to have, use and enjoy, a right of way to and from the said land, called Tavern, otherwise Guildhall hill, for the purpose of observing vessels coming to or going from the Harbour of Blakeney aforesaid, or otherwise passing or repassing upon the high seas'.

this port 102 coasting vessels register 4,930 tons' (White's 1890), this was tempered by, 'but the coasting trade, once considerable is now, in 1888, rapidly declining (Kelly's 1888). Twelve years later, they were able to pronounce that: 'This was formerly a port called Blakeney and Cley' (Kelly's 1900).[18]

1909–11   In 1909, having been a familiar sight at Blakeney quay for over 42 years, the *Bluejacket* suffered the indignity of having her masts removed and being converted to a lighter, being towed by the tug *Comet*. She was a billyboy ketch of 57 tons built at Walsoken in 1860 but, from 1867, traded regularly from Blakeney, owned successively by the Breretons, the Parkers and Page and Turner. She proved too big and cumbersome to be a successful lighter and, in 1911, was converted into a houseboat. She remained a familiar landmark until she finally rotted away on Morston marshes in 1932.[19]

It is impossible to say when the last vessel traded at either Blakeney or Cley. The evidence is anecdotal. Peter Catling believed that the *New Walter and Ann* was the last vessel to trade at Cley although he gives no date. Elsewhere he has said that the last cargo to Cley was offloaded from lighters in 1905.

The *Taffy* and the *Jessie* were still trading from Blakeney in 1913 and, Blakeney resident, Sam Parsons believed that the barges *Alert* and *Sir James Carfield* were the last ships to arrive at Blakeney to unload granite chips for the roads. No date was given but the Blakeney Harbour Company was wound up around 1914. Peter Catling also stated that the last sea going vessel belonging to Blakeney was sold in 1916 and that the last cargo to Blakeney quay was a shipment of cattle cake that arrived in 1923.[20] Others claimed it was the *Angerona* (see plate 9) but a letter from Herbert Starling to the *Eastern Daily Press*

Plate 38: Martin Page (left) and Clifford Turner (right), the last major merchants and ship owners.

written on 7 December 1928 disagreed. He said he well remembered the *Angerona* that had been featured in the last Saturday's issue and said it was not the last vessel to discharge at Cley quay. He continued, 'I cannot remember the name of this Norwegian vessel which was laden with timber and discharged its cargo opposite the old granary since used by the Salvation Army…This vessel was there some days after unloading as the tides were low, and on leaving early one morning it grounded near the 'Steeps' about half way down the channel and remained there until the tides were bigger. This was the last to visit Cley.'

1922

If any year marks the final end of trade it is probably 1922. The last few cargoes had been carried for, and in, ships belonging to Page and Turner. In October of that yea,r they finally closed their remaining granaries in Blakeney and transferred their business to Holt, on the rail network. The report of this move in the *Eastern Daily Press* was entitled "The passing of a port". The newspaper also reported that the lingering trade finally ceased when a 'stranger' made an offer for the remaining ships and 'one fine day' the remnants of Page and Turner's fleet sailed away. It is a pity that the reporter did not inform his readership about 'who' and 'when' but he did sum up, if somewhat poetically, the final decline and it is worth quoting at length.

Seventy years ago business in both parishes was in full swing; the harbour had its staff of pilots, who were kept busy with outgoing and incoming vessels and the quay sides were lined with shipping, the export and import trades being of considerable dimensions. In those days the Customs House was established at Cley and the tide waiters were in constant request, the Baltic trade and the foreign coasting trade warranting more than local fame. At that period over seventy sailing vessels with three hundred fishing boats belonged to the port. From early morning wagons from remote parts of the countryside were pouring their freights into the granaries and carrying back feeding stuffs and coals. Every inch of accommodation was taken up by the horses, and the lines of wagons extended far into the streets. Quite a fourth of the adult population were employed manning the ships or discharging and loading cargoes at the quay.[21]

1923

The following year the *Blakeney Hotel* was built on the quay. Two cottages, the *Crown and Anchor* public house (known locally as the Barking Dickey), a coal merchant's house and a brewery and maltings were demolished to make way for the hotel. The last vestiges of the port finally disappeared—the hotel symbolically represented the triumph of tourism and pleasure boating over trade. This would now form the basis for the local economy throughout the 20th century and up to the present day.

Though Blakeney and Cley now showed little sign of ever being a thriving port, there is still some evidence, hidden away, that hints at their former glory and can be found in the evidence boxes scattered through the text.

Notes

1   Jefferson, R (2002) The William & Thomas Trading Accounts (1726–1733) in *The Glaven Historian* no. 5 Blakeney pp. 58–65.

2   NRO MC 284/4XT 200E Cley-next-the-Sea Parish Registers vol. 5.

3   Bryce, Maj A Report on the Coast of Norfolk, more particularly from Happisburgh to Hunstanton reprinted in Bird, M.(2013) *The Diary of Mary Hardy* vol. 4 Kingston-upon-Thames, Appendix D4.C p. 467; NRO MC 284/1–4.

4   An Act for Improving the Harbour of Blakeney 57 Geo III chLXX; Hooton JJ (1996) *The Glaven Ports* Blakeney, Blakeney History Group ch. 34.

5   House of Lords Record Office (HLRO) 2nd Report of the Tidal Harbours Commission in Sessional Papers 1846 [692] [746] XVIII Appendix p. 468.

6   Palmer, HR Plan of Cley & Blakeney in Norfolk reproduced in the Appendix of HLRO 2nd Report of the Tidal Harbours Commission in Sessional Papers 1846 [692] [756] XVIII.

7   Hooton JJ (1996) *The Glaven Ports* Blakeney, Blakeney History Group ch. 32 pp. 213–27.

8   NRO P/SH/L/10 no. 8 1839; NRO P/SH/L/10 no. 2 1845; Hooton, JJ (2003) The Ann of Clay Capt. Francis Plumb 1841 in *The Glaven Historian* no. 6 p. 15.

9   NRO P/SH/L/10 no. 4 1842; NRO Bowden-Smith papers Q199A.

10   ibid., 5 xviii parts 1 and 2 and Appendix A.

11   Custome & Excise Library General Letters 1853 no. 32.

12   ibid., 7 ch. 32 pp. 220–27.

13   Hooton, JJ (2018) William Allen: Weybourne ship owner in *The Glaven Historian* no. 16 p. 45.

14   ibid., 7 ch. 39 pp. 276–80.

15   ibid., 7 ch. 35 pp. 241–44; HLRO Lynn& Fakenham Railway Act 1882 45 & 46 (Vict).

16   Hooper, J (1905) *Nelson's homeland* Homeland Association Ltd, London pp. 156–7.

17   Harman, W J (1995) ed. Walker, GB *The Memoirs of William John Harman 1854–1944* Walker, Wells p. 39; personal communication in a taped interview with Sam Parsons (aged 83) Blakeney resident, April 1980 author's collection.

18   *White's Norfolk Directory 1890*; *Kelly's Directory of Norfolk 1888 and 1900*.

19   ibid., 7 ch. 36 pp. 249–51; East, S (2018) The Billyboy Ketch Bluejacket in *The Glaven Historian* no. 16 p. 54.

20   Catling, M (c.1960–80) *History of Blakeney and its Havens* Mss. Norfolk Heritage Library; Catling M and Stangroom, J *Trading History of Blakeney and Cley* unpublished mss author's collection; Parsons, S taped interview ibid., 17 author's collection.

21   *Eastern Daily Press* 19 October 1922.

8: The Last Vessels

FROM the end of the 19th century and the start of the 20th, photographic evidence of the port and her vessels has survived. As an epilogue, this last chapter will look at some of the final vessels to trade from the Glaven using the photographs that remain, in the hope that this will give a feel for this former port with a worthy past.

One of the vessels to feature in a great deal in the photographs is the *Comet*. This was not surprising as she was the port's tug, used for towing vessels or lighters up to, and away from, the quay—a constant presence at the port. She was by no means the first harbour tug. That honour belongs to the *Premier* which arrived in 1838. She was replaced with the *Gem*, and then the *Patriot*, both paddle tugs. The *Comet* was built in 1889 by William Cook at Middlesbrough and started working for Allen Brown Ltd at Newcastle. In 1897, she was bought by Edward Clifford Turner, part of the fleet belonging to Page and Turner, corn merchants based at Blakeney. She was a permanent feature of the port until sold in 1916 to Great Yarmouth and then to London, before ending back up in Middlesbrough. The *Comet* was a steam screw propelled tug with a tonnage of 29 tons. James Newland was her first master and later she was skippered by John Butters and lastly by Ted Buck.[1]

Most of the fleet that operated out of Blakeney by the second half of the 19th century were second hand ships. Many of them did not last very long, two fifths of all vessels on the register at Cley and Wells from 1867 were lost and few lasted longer than 20 years. However, the *Minstrel* was built locally, in

Comet

Minstrel

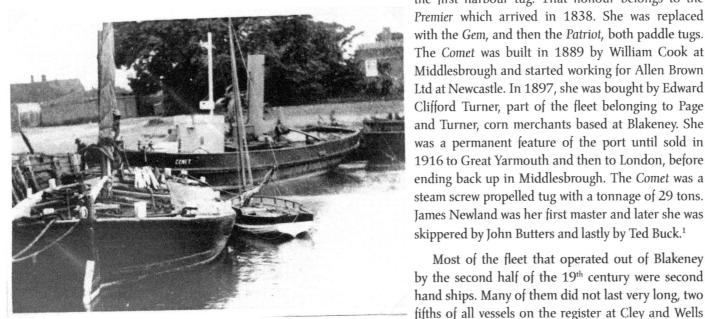

Plate 39: Comet, with her distinctive buff coloured funnel, moored at the western end of the quay, behind one of the Blakeney lighters, probably 'Clam'.

1847, at Wells and served the north Norfolk ports for 57 years before she became stranded, in 1904, on the Lincolnshire coast during an easterly gale. Abandoned, she was broken up in situ. She was a top sail schooner of 65 tons built by Henry Tyrrel in his shipyard for Thomas Thirtle Mack of Burnham Thorpe. She traded regularly out of Burnham and Wells carrying grain and malt from Norfolk, returning with coal and cattle cake from the north. There were also several trips to Germany and the Baltic.

Her first two masters were Henry Howell and then his son. In 1891 she was sold and came under the control of William Temple. He had been born in Wells, but was increasingly sailing the *Minstrel* from various ports, including Blakeney. By the start of the 20th century she had to go where there were cargoes. In 1901, she made 36 journeys from numerous ports ranging from Sunderland in the north, to Cowes and Southampton in the south, only coming to Blakeney four times. The nature of the crew had changed as well. In the early years they were all local men from north Norfolk, but by 1901 only Temple, the master, was local, being described as 'from Wells' sometimes and 'Blakeney' at others. The rest of the crew (mate, ordinary seaman and cook) came from a variety of places in the UK and abroad. In 1901, *Minstrel* ended her days laid up in Wintringham, on the Humber, for repairs.[2]

Plate 40: Minstrel unloading at Blakeney at Gus Hill's Quay—the New Walter and Ann can be seen in the background.

Bluejacket

Bluejacket is a ship that was synonymous with Blakeney. The reason she was so well remembered was that at the end of her life she was converted into a houseboat (1911) remaining on the Morston marshes until the 1930s where she eventually rotted away. Michael Stammers in *Victorian North Norfolk Sailing Ships* stated that she was named after an 18th century Shawnee chief whose name had also been used for a famous American clipper in 1854.

Plate 41: Model of Bluejacket by Peter Catling.

Peter Catling made the model of *Bluejacket* illustrated here (plate 41). He took detailed measurements of the rotting hull as a basis for the model. His research also included studying paintings and photographs of her and talking to the old seamen, still in Blakeney in the 1930s, who had known the vessel or sailed in her. She was a ketch of 57 tons, built at Walsoken in 1860 and started sailing out of Wisbech, before being bought by the Blakeney merchant Benjamin Nichols in 1868. He sold her on to Page and Turner in 1878 and she became a regular trader out of Blakeney. In 1909, Page and Turner removed her masts and used her as a lighter, pulled by *Comet*. However, too cumbersome to make a successful lighter, two years later she was sold, initially to the Cozens-Hardy's and, later, to the Hamonds to be converted into a houseboat. 'Gundy' Holman, who sailed in her, is reputed to have said, 'She'll starve you, but never drown you'. Indeed she had a successful 51 years of service before becoming a houseboat.[3]

Plate 42: Bluejacket as a lighter.

Plate 43: Bluejacket near the end of her life on the Morston marshes.

Mary Ann

The *Mary Ann* was a 47 ton ketch built in Whitstable in 1832. Previously she had been registered at Faversham but came 'off register' after being wrecked. When she was re-registered at Lynn in 1882, it was recorded that she had a certificate of seaworthiness and joined the Page and Turner fleet. In 1896 the ownership was transferred solely to Edward Clifford Turner and, in 1908, the risk was more evenly spread when Ellis Capps Turner and Alfred Edward Turner became joint owners. Alfred Edward Turner was killed in action in October 1915 and Edward Clifford Turner died in July 1916. It left Ellis Capps as the sole owner. He passed the ship on to a Yarmouth shipbroker in 1917. The registry was finally closed in April 1923 when she was broken up after an amazing 91 years of service. A painting of her was photographed before it was sold at auction and hangs in Blakeney village hall. Peter Catling had an extract from the log of the *Mary Ann* for 7–10 August 1910 which provides an example of some of the problems faced by these older ships:

> Arrived at Blakeney Quay at 8 am from Hull loaded with 38 tons Linseed Cakes & 47 tons Cotton Cakes, vessel tight and all right. At 10.00 am vessel listed off from the quay and on the night flood at about 7 o'clock made a lot of water and although the pump was constantly kept going she damaged the cargo, Keelson deep—soon as vessel floated the leak stopped and having shifted to next berth she has been tight ever since. (signed) J Broughton his X mark (Master).

Page and Turner requested a report, which was carried out by John Butters and Robert Pells (2 master mariners) who stated that only about 12 tons were seriously damaged and added that: 'in order to avoid further loss, we recommend the vessel to be discharged as quickly as possible and the damaged cakes to be disposed of before they have time to heat'. The *Mary Ann* continued to trade for another 10 years—a tribute to the way the local seamen were able to repair and keep their old vessels seaworthy. A further entry in the log stated: 'Started work 6 am to lighten vessel and to avoid further damage. 10.30 had surveyors who advised quick discharge which is proceeding'. Again

Plate 44: This shot of the quay shows Mary Ann in the middle behind Bluejacket and in front of some of the lighters.

Plate 45: 'Mary Ann' at the west end of Blakeney Quay.

Plate 46: The steamship 'Taffy' berthed and maybe stuck at Blakeney Quay.

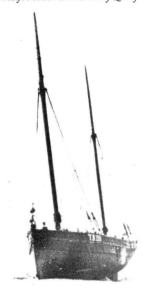

Plate 47: 'Sir John Colomb' when still a drifter ashore on Blakeney Point.

the master put his mark, the whole proceedings being witnessed by E Stearman, who was the Merchant's Clerk, presumably working for Page and Turner.[4]

Taffy

The *Taffy* was a little different in that she was a steamship. With a gross tonnage of 172 tons, she was too large to reach the quay unless she had been part unloaded by lighters at anchor in the Pit. She was built at Port Glasgow in 1894 and was first registered at Runcorn in Cheshire. Edward Clifford Turner bought her in December 1898. Selling a lot of shares in the vessel, he was left with just 27 out of the original 64. Loads Thompson, who had two shares, was the master of the vessel. There is a village tradition (as well as photographic evidence) that she did come up to the Quay once, but was then stuck there for a month before there was a tide high enough to refloat her. According to Blakeney resident, Sam Parsons, she largely made trips to Leith and Sunderland taking barley to the Vaux brewery, but sometimes went to Mistley in Essex and occasionally France. Eventually, in July 1913, she was sold to the Rix brothers, shipowners from Hull. There was still a local connection, Robert Rix having been born in Wells.[5]

Sir John Colomb

Sir John Colomb was an ex-herring drifter YH218 built by Beechings at Yarmouth in 1896. She was named after the naval strategist who became MP for Great Yarmouth from 1895 to 1906. She ran aground on Blakeney Point somewhere between the Watch House and the Hood in thick fog on 17 August 1909. Page and Turner bought her and had the vessel winched off the Point and towed round into the harbour. Here her keel was repaired and she was added to the Page and Turner fleet. Her master was Mr Greene with Sam Breeze as his mate. For Page and Turner this was a cheap and effective way of building up and maintaining a fleet. Page and Turner were described as maltsters, cake, coal and general merchants who also owned a farm at Morston and had offices at Holt and Brancaster. They ceased trading from Blakeney sometime during the First World War moving their business to Holt in 1922. Their ships always had a distinctive white band painted around their hulls.[6]

New Walter and Ann

The *New Walter and Ann* was a 30 ton lugger built at Yarmouth and worked as a fishing vessel for Christopher West of Sheringham. In 1879, she was converted to a ketch and sold to William Temple. He started to trade with her out of Blakeney. This continued until the end of 1903 when her registry was closed and she was broken up.[7]

This brief look at some of the last vessels to trade from Blakeney, hopefully, gives colour to the facts and paints a more complete picture of the port of Blakeney.

Plate 48: Painting of 'Sir John Colomb' when part of the Page and Turner fleet.

The town, even before the First World War, was becoming popular with artists, ornithologists and holiday makers. Blakeney was changing— leisure becoming the main income generator rather than shipping. This trend had already started at Cley, where wildfowling was replacing maritime trade and this accelerated after the First World War. Naturalists had long been interested in the area and, encouraged by Professor Frank Oliver, who had bought the Old Lifeboat House in 1910 to become a base for research, building a laboratory there some three years later. Professor Oliver's enthusiasm led to Blakeney Point being bought and handed over to the National Trust as a nature reserve. This set the scene for the former port's future importance and financial stability.[8]

Plate 49: 'New Walter and Ann' at the east end of the quay.

Notes

1   Tyne & Wear Archives Service (TWAS) 2870 B385F.

2   Hooton, JJ (2005) Minstrel Biography of a sailing ship in *The Glaven Historian* no. 8 p. 3.

3   Catling, M (1965) The Bluejacket in the Norfolk Sailor no. 10; Hooton, JJ (2007) The Catling Ship Models in *The Glaven Historian* no. 10 p. 23.

4   Norfolk Heritage Centre Report of Damage to Mary Ann in Catling, M (compiler) Collection of Photographs & other material relating to Blakeney & Cley; NRO P/SH/L/4.

5   Cheshire Record Office (CRO) NR 4098/141; personal communication in a taped interview with Sam Parsons (aged 83) Blakeney resident, April 1980 author's collection.

6   Parsons, S Taped interview, author's collection; James Steward, Great Yarmouth Museums personal commnunication.

7   Parsons, S Taped interview, author's collection; Stammers, M (2012) *Victorian North Norfolk Sailing Ships* Milepost Research p. 43.

8   Oliver, F. & Carey, AE (1918) Tidal Lands: a Study of Shore problems part of which was reproduced in Peake, J (2012) *Blakeney Point: From the Point to Cley & Salthouse* History Centre, Blakeney.

Index